The Constitution of
The State of Nebraska:
A Quick Reference Guide

Bootblack Budget Books
Copyright 2018 ©
ISBN-13: 978-1987655315
ISBN-10: 1987655311

Contents:

Preamble – Page 27

Article I: Bill of Rights – Page 28

Section 1. Statement of Rights

Section 2. Slavery Prohibited

Section 3. Due Process of Law; Equal Protection

Section 4. Religious Freedom.

Section 5. Freedom of Speech And Press

Section 6. Trial by Jury

Section 7. Search and Seizure

Section 8. Habeas Corpus

Section 9. Bail; Fines; Imprisonment; Cruel and Unusual Punishment

Section 10. Presentment or Indictment by Grand Jury; Information

Section 11. Rights of Accused

Section 12. Evidence Against Self; Double Jeopardy

Section 13. Justice Administered Without Delay; Legislature; Authorization to Enforce Mediation And Arbitration

Section 14. Treason

Section 15. Penalties; Corruption of Blood; Transporting Out of State Prohibited

Section 16. Bill Of Attainder; Retroactive Laws; Contracts; Special Privileges

Section 17. Military Subordinate

Section 18. Soldiers Quarters

Section 19. Right of Peaceable Assembly and to Petition Government

Section 20. Imprisonment for Debt Prohibited

Section 21. Private Property Compensated For

Section 22. Elections to be Free

Section 23. Capital Cases; Right of Direct Appeal; Effect; Other Cases; Right of Appeal

Section 24. Repealed

Section 25. Rights of Property; No Discrimination; Aliens

Section 26. Powers Retained by People

Section 27. English Language to be Official

Section 28. Crime Victims; Rights Enumerated; Effect; Legislature; Duties

Section 29. Marriage; Same-Sex Relationships Not Valid or Recognized

Section 30. Discrimination or Grant Of Preferential Treatment Prohibited; Public Employment, Public Education, or Public Contracting; Section, How Construed; Remedies

Article II: Distribution of Powers – Page 37

Section 1. Legislative, Executive, Judicial

Article III: Legislative – Page 38

Section 1. Legislative Authority; How Vested; Power of Initiative; Power of Referendum

Section 2. First Power Reserved; Initiative

Section 3. Second Power Reserved; Referendum

Section 4. Initiative or Referendum; Signatures Required; Veto; Election Returns; Constitutional Amendments; Non-Partisan Ballot

Section 5. Legislative Districts; Apportionment; Redistricting, When Required

Section 6. Legislature; Number of Members; Annual Sessions

Section 7. Legislators; Terms; Effect of Redistricting; Election; Salary; Expenses; Mileage

Section 8. Legislators; Qualifications; One-Year Residence n District; Removal From District, Effect

Section 9. Legislators; Disqualifications; Election to Other Office; Resignation Required

Section 10. Legislative Sessions; Time; Quorum; Rules of Procedure; Expulsion of Members; Disrespectful Behavior, Penalty

Section 11. Legislative Journal; Vote Viva Voce; Open Doors; Committee Votes

Section 12. Legislators; Terms; Limitation

Section 13. Style Of Bills; Majority Necessary to Passage; Yeas and Nays Entered on Journal

Section 14. Bills and Resolutions Read by Title; Printing; Vote For Final Passage; Bills To Contain One Subject; Amended Section To Be Set Forth; Signing of Bills

Section 15. Members Privileged From Arrest

Section 16. Members of The Legislature And State Officers; Conflicts Of Interest; Standards For

Section 17. Impeachment; Procedure

Section 18. Local or Special Laws Prohibited

Section 19. Compensation; Increase When; Extra Compensation to Public Officers and Contractors Prohibited; Retirement Benefits; Adjustment

Section 20. Salt Springs, Coal, Oil, Minerals; Alienation Prohibited

Section 21. Donation of State Lands Prohibited; When

Section 22. Appropriations For State; Deficiencies; Bills for Pay Of Members And Officials

Section 23. Repealed

Section 24. Games of Chance, Lotteries, and Gift Enterprises; Restrictions; Parimutuel Wagering on Horse races; Bingo Games; Use of State Lottery Proceeds

Section 25. Incidental Expenses of State Officers; Specific Appropriations Always Necessary; Warrants for Money

Section 26. Privilege of Members

Section 27. Acts Take Effect After Three Months; Emergency Bills; Session Laws

Section 28. Repealed

Section 29. Legislative Authority in Emergencies Due to Enemy Attack Upon United States

Section 30. Legislature to Pass Necessary Laws

Article IV: Executive – Page 56

Section 1. Executive Departments; Officers; When Elected; Terms; Eligibility; Books to be Kept at Seat of Government; Residence of Officers; Heads of Departments; Appointments

Section 2. Governor; Lieutenant Governor; Eligibility; Qualifications; Appointive Officers, Ineligible for Other Office

Section 3. Treasurer; Ineligibility

Section 4. Election Returns; Canvass by Legislature; Conduct Election Contests

Section 5. Impeachment

Section 6. Supreme Executive Power

Section 7. Message by Governor; Budget; Contents; Budget Bill; Preparation; Appropriations not to be in Excess Budget; Exception; Excess Subject to Veto

Section 8. Special Sessions

Section 9. Repealed

Section 10. Governor to Appoint Officers; Removal

Section 11. Elected State Officer; Vacation Office; Governor Fill by Appointment; Term

Section 12. Nonelective State Officers; Vacation; Governor; Fill the Office by Appointment; Approval by Legislature

Section 13. Board of Parole; Members; Powers; Reprieves; Proceedings; Power to Pardon; Limitations

Section 14. Governor to be Commander-in-Chief Militia

Section 15. Bills to be Presented to Governor; Approval; Procedure; Disapproval or Reduction Items Appropriation; Passage Despite Disapproval or Reduction

Section 16. Order Succession to Become Governor; Lieutenant Governor; Duties

Section 17. Repealed

Section 18. Repealed

Section 19. State Institutions; Management, Control, And Government; Determination by Legislature

Section 20. Public Service Commission; Membership; Terms; Powers

Section 21. Repealed

Section 22. Executive Officials to Keep Accounts; Reports; False Reports, Penalty

Section 23. Executive Officials and Heads Institutions; Reports to Legislature; Information From Expending Agencies

Section 24. Great Seal

Section 25. Salaries Officials; Fees

Section 26. Officials to Give Bonds

Section 27. Executive Offices; Creation

Section 28. Tax Equalization and Review Commission; Members; Powers; Tax Commissioner; Powers

Article V: Judicial – Page 66

Section 1. Power Vested in Courts; Chief Justice; Powers

Section 2. Supreme Court; Number of Judges; Quorum; Jurisdiction; Retired Judges, Temporary Duty; Court Divisions; Assignments by Chief Justice

Section 3. Terms of Supreme Court

Section 4. Chief Justice and Judges of The Supreme Court; Selection; Residence; Location of Offices

Section 5. Supreme Court Judicial Districts; Redistricting; When

Section 6. Chief Justice to Preside

Section 7. Chief Justice; Associate Justices; Qualifications

Section 8. Supreme Court Appoint Staff; Budget; Copyright of State Reports

Section 9. District Courts; Jurisdiction; Felons May Plead Guilty; Sentence

Section 10. District Court Judicial Districts

Section 11. District Court Judges; Change of Number; Boundaries

Section 12. District Court Judges May Hold Court for Each Other; Retired Judges, Temporary Duty

Section 13. Supreme and District Judges; Salaries

Section 14. Supreme and District Judges not to Act as Attorneys; Judge not to Practice Law, When

Section 15. Repealed

Section 16. Repealed

Section 17. Repealed

Section 18. Repealed

Section 19. Practice of All Courts to be Uniform

20. Officers in This Article; Tenure; Residence; Duties; Compensation

Section 21. Merit Plan for Selection of Judges; Terms of Office; Filling of Vacancies; Procedure; Voting for Nominee

Section 22. State May Sue and be Sued

Section 23. Jurisdiction of Judges at Chambers

Section 24. Style of Process

Section 25. Supreme Court to Promulgate Rules of Practice; to Make Recommendations to Legislature

Section 26. Proviso as to Effect of Amendment

Section 27. Juvenile Courts; Authorization

Section 28. Commission On Judicial Qualifications; Appointment; Composition; Qualifications

Section 29. Commission on Judicial Qualifications; Vote Of Majority Required for Action

Section 30. Judges; Discipline; Removal From Office; Grounds; Procedure

Section 31. Judges; Procedure for Removal From Office Cumulative

Article VI: Suffrage – Page 80

Section 1. Qualifications of Electors

Section 2. Who Disqualified

Section 3. Military or Naval Service; Place And Manner of Voting

Section 4. Repealed

Section 5. Electors; Privileged From Arrest

Section 6. Votes, How Cast

Article VII: Education – Page 81

Section 1. Legislature; Free Instruction in Common Schools; Provide

Section 2. State Department of Education; General Supervision of School System

Section 3. State Board of Education; Members; Election; Manner of Election; Term Of Office

Section 4. State Board of Education; Commissioner of Education; Appointment; Powers; Duties

Section 5. Fines, Penalties, and License Money; Allocation; Use of Forfeited Conveyances

Section 6. Educational Lands; Management; Board of Educational Lands and Funds; Members; Appointment; Sale of Lands

Section 7. Perpetual Funds Enumerated

Section 8. Trust Funds Belong to State for Educational Purposes; Use; Investment

Section 9. Educational Funds; Trust Funds; Use; Early Childhood Education Endowment Fund; Created; Use; Early Childhood Education, Defined

Section 10. University Of Nebraska; Government; Board of Regents; Election; Student Membership; Terms

Section 11. Appropriation of Public Funds; Handicapped Children; Sectarian Instruction; Religious Test of Teacher or Student

Section 12. Education and Reform of Minors

Section 13. State Colleges; Government; Board; Name; Selection; Duties; Compensation

Section 14. Coordinating Commission For Postsecondary Education; Membership; Powers and Duties; Coordination, Defined

Section 15. Omitted

Section 16. Repealed

Section 17. Repealed

Article VIII: Revenue – Page 91

Section 1. Revenue; Raised by Taxation; Legislative Powers

Section 1a. Levy of Property Tax for State Purposes; Prohibition

Section 1b. Income Tax; May be Based Upon the Laws of the United States

Section 2. Exemption of Property From Taxation; Classification

Section 2a. Exemption of Personal Property in Transit in Licensed Warehouses or Storage Areas

Section 3. Redemption From Sales of Real Estate for Taxes

Section 4. Legislature Has no Power to Remit Taxes; Exception; Cancellation of Taxes on Land Acquired by the State

Section 5. County Taxes; Limitation

Section 6. Local Improvements of Cities, Towns and Villages

Section 7. Private Property Not Liable for Corporate Debts; Municipalities and Inhabitants Exempt for Corporate Purposes

Section 8. Funding Indebtedness; Warrants

Section 9. Claims Upon Treasury; Adjustment; Approval; Appeal

Section 10. Taxation of Grain And Seed; Alternative Basis Permitted

Section 11. Public Corporations and Political Subdivisions Providing Electricity; Payment in Lieu of Taxes

Section 12. Cities or Villages; Redevelopment Project; Substandard and Blighted Property; Incur Indebtedness; Taxes; How Treated

Section 13. Revenue Laws And Legislative Acts; How Construed

Article IX: Counties – Page 100

Section 1. Area

Section 2. Division of County; Decision of Question

Section 3. County Added to Another; Prior Indebtedness; County Stricken Off; Liabilities

Section 4. County and Township Officers

Section 5. Township Organization

Article X: Public Service Corporations – Page 102

Section 1. Reports Under Oath

Section 2. Property Liable to Sale on Execution

Section 3. Consolidation of Stock or Property

Section 4. Railways Declared Public Highways; Maximum Rates; Liability Not Limited

Section 5. Capital Stock; Dividends

Section 6. Eminent Domain

Section 7. Unjust Discrimination and Extortion

Section 8. Eminent Domain for Depot or Other Uses

Article XI: Municipal Corporations – Page 105

Section 1. Subscription to Stock Prohibited; Exception

Section 2. City Of 5,000 May Frame Charter; Procedure

Section 3. Rejection Of Charter; Effect; Procedure to Frame New Charter

Section 4. Charter; Amendment; Charter Convention

Section 5. Charter of City Of 100,000; Home Rule Charter Authorized

Article XII: Miscellaneous Corporations – Page **109**

Section 1. Legislature to Provide for Organization, Regulation, and Supervision of Corporations and Associations; Limitation; Elections for Directors or Managers; Voting Rights of Stockholders

Section 2. Repealed

Section 3. Repealed

Section 4. Repealed

Section 5. Repealed

Section 6. Repealed

Section 7. Repealed

Section 8. Corporation Acquiring an Interest in Real Estate Used for Farming or Ranching or Engaging in Farming or Ranching; Restrictions; Secretary of State, Attorney General; Duties; Legislature; Powers

Article XIII: State, County, and Municipal Indebtedness – Page 115

Section 1. State May Contract Debts; Limitation; Exceptions

Section 2. Industrial and Economic Development; Powers of Counties and Municipalities

Section 3. Credit of State; Exception

Section 4. Nonprofit Enterprise Development; Powers of Counties and Municipalities

Article XIV: Militia – Page 118

Section 1. Personnel; Organization; Discipline

Article XV: Miscellaneous Provisions – Page 119

Section 1. Official Oath; Refusal; Disqualification

Section 2. Official in Default as Collector and Custodian of Public Money or Property; Disqualification; Felon Disqualified

Section 3. Repealed

Section 4. Water a Public Necessity

Section 5. Use of Water Dedicated to People

Section 6. Right to Divert Unappropriated Waters

Section 7. Use of Water for Power Purposes

Section 8. Employment of Women and Children; Minimum Wage

Section 9. Controversies Between Employers and Employees; Industrial Commission; Appeals

Section 10. Repealed

Section 11. Repealed

Section 12. Removal of State Capital

Section 13. Labor Organizations; no Denial of Employment; Closed Shop not Permitted

Section 14. Labor Organization; Definition

Section 15. Labor Organizations; Amendment Self-Executing; Laws to Facilitate Operation Permitted

Section 16. Repealed

Section 17. Retirement and Pension Funds; Investment

Section 18. Governmental Powers and Functions; Intergovernmental Cooperation; Legislature May Limit; Merger or Consolidation of Counties or Other Local Governments Authorized

Section 19. Liquor Licenses; Municipalities and Counties; Powers

Section 20. Omitted

Section 21. Omitted

Section 22. Omitted

Section 23. Omitted

Section 24. Omitted

Section 25. Right to Hunt, to Fish, and to Harvest Wildlife; Public Hunting, Fishing, and Harvesting of Wildlife; Preferred Means of Managing and Controlling Wildlife

Article XVI: Amendments – Page 125

Section 1. How Proposed

Section 2. Convention

Article XVII: Schedule – Page 127

Section 1. Terms; Reference to Members of the Legislature to Include Appointed And Elected Members

Section 2. Repealed

Section 3. Repealed

Section 4. General Election of State

Section 5. Terms of Office of All Elected Officers

Section 6. Transferred to Article III, Section 30, Constitution of f Nebraska

Section 7. Repealed

Section 8. Repealed

Section 9. Repealed

Section 10. Sec. 10. (Failed to Carry at Election.)

Section 11. Repealed

Article XVIII: Term Limits on Congress – Page 129

Section 1. Statement of Intent

Section 2. Instruction to Members of Congressional Delegation; Ballot Notation; When

Section 3. Nonincumbent Candidates; Term Limits Pledge; Ballot Notation; When

Section 4. Instruction to Members of the Legislature; Ballot Notation; When

Section 5. Ballot Notation; Secretary Of State; Duties; Appeal

Section 6. Automatic Repeal; When

Section 7. Legal Challenge; Jurisdiction

Section 8. Severability

Preamble:

We, the people, grateful to Almighty God for our freedom, do ordain and establish the following declaration of rights and frame of government, as the Constitution of the State of Nebraska.

Article I: Bill of Rights

Section 1: Statement of Rights

All persons are by nature free and independent, and have certain inherent and inalienable rights; among these are life, liberty, the pursuit of happiness, and the right to keep and bear arms for security or defense of self, family, home, and others, and for lawful common defense, hunting, recreational use, and all other lawful purposes, and such rights shall not be denied or infringed by the state or any subdivision thereof. To secure these rights, and the protection of property, governments are instituted among people, deriving their just powers from the consent of the governed.

Section 2: Slavery Prohibited

There shall be neither slavery nor involuntary servitude in this state, otherwise than for punishment of crime, whereof the party shall have been duly convicted.

Section 3: Due Process of Law; Equal Protection

No person shall be deprived of life, liberty, or property, without due process of law, nor be denied equal protection of the laws.

Section 4: Religious Freedom

All persons have a natural and indefeasible right to worship Almighty God according to the dictates of their own consciences. No person shall be compelled to attend, erect or support any place of worship against his consent, and no preference shall be given by law to any religious society, nor shall any interference with the rights of conscience be permitted. No religious test shall be required as a qualification for office, nor shall any person be incompetent to be a witness on account of his religious beliefs; but nothing herein shall be construed to dispense with oaths and affirmations. Religion, morality, and knowledge, however, being essential to good government, it shall be the duty of the Legislature to pass suitable laws to protect every religious denomination in the peaceable enjoyment of its own mode of public worship, and to encourage schools and the means of instruction.

Section 5. Freedom of Speech and Press

Every person may freely speak, write and publish on all subjects, being responsible for the abuse of that liberty; and in all trials for libel, both civil and criminal, the truth when published with good motives, and for justifiable ends, shall be a sufficient defense.

6: Trial by Jury

The right of trial by jury shall remain inviolate, but the Legislature may authorize trial by a jury of a less number than twelve in courts inferior to the District Court, and may by general law authorize a verdict in civil cases in any court by not less than five-sixths of the jury.

Section 7. Search and Seizure

The right of the people to be secure in their persons, houses, papers, and effects against unreasonable searches and seizures shall not be violated; and no warrant shall issue but upon probable cause, supported by oath or affirmation, and particularly describing the place to be searched, and the person or thing to be seized.

Section 8. Habeas Corpus

The privilege of the writ of habeas corpus shall not be suspended.

Section 9. Bail; Fines; Imprisonment; Cruel and Unusual Punishment

All persons shall be bailable by sufficient sureties, except for treason, sexual offenses involving penetration by force or against the will of the victim, and murder, where the proof is evident or the presumption great. Excessive bail shall not be required, nor excessive fines imposed, nor cruel and unusual punishment inflicted.

Section 10. Presentment or Indictment by Grand Jury; Information

No person shall be held to answer for a criminal offense, except in cases in which the punishment is by fine, or imprisonment otherwise than in the penitentiary, in case of impeachment, and in cases arising in the army and navy, or in the militia when in actual service in time of war or public danger, unless on a presentment or indictment of a grand jury; Provided, That the Legislature may by law provide for holding persons to answer for criminal offenses on information of a public prosecutor; and may by law, abolish, limit, change, amend, or otherwise regulate the grand jury system.

Section 11. Rights of Accused

In all criminal prosecutions the accused shall have the right to appear and defend in person or by counsel, to demand the nature and cause of accusation, and to have a copy thereof; to meet the witnesses against him face to face; to have process to compel the attendance of witnesses in his behalf; and a speedy public trial by an impartial jury of the county or district in which the offense is alleged to have been committed.

Section 12. Evidence Against Self; Double Jeopardy

No person shall be compelled, in any criminal case, to give evidence against himself, or be twice put in jeopardy for the same offense.

Section 13. Justice Administered without Delay; Legislature; Authorization to Enforce Mediation and Arbitration

All courts shall be open, and every person, for any injury done him or her in his or her lands, goods, person, or reputation, shall have a remedy by due course of law and justice administered without denial or delay, except that the Legislature may provide for the enforcement of mediation, binding arbitration agreements, and other forms of dispute resolution which are entered into voluntarily and which are not revocable other than upon such grounds as exist at law or in equity for the revocation of any contract.

Section 14. Treason

Treason against the state shall consist only in levying war against the state, or in adhering to its enemies, giving them aid and comfort. No person shall be convicted of treason unless on the testimony of two witnesses to the same overt act, or on confession in open court.

Section 15. Penalties; Corruption of Blood; Transporting out of State Prohibited

All penalties shall be proportioned to the nature of the offense, and no conviction shall work corruption of blood or forfeiture of estate; nor shall any person be transported out of the state for any offense committed within the state.

Section 16. Bill of Attainder; Retroactive Laws; Contracts; Special Privileges

No bill of attainder, ex post facto law, or law impairing the obligation of contracts, or making any irrevocable grant of special privileges or immunities shall be passed.

Section 17. Military Subordinate

The military shall be in strict subordination to the civil power.

Section 18. Soldiers Quarters

No soldier shall in time of peace be quartered in any house without the consent of the owner; nor in time of war except in the manner prescribed by law.

Section 19. Right of peaceable assembly and to petition government.

The right of the people peaceably to assemble to consult for the common good, and to petition the government, or any department thereof, shall never be abridged.

Section 20. Imprisonment for Debt Prohibited

No person shall be imprisoned for debt in any civil action on mesne or final process.

Section 21. Private Property Compensated for

The property of no person shall be taken or damaged for public use without just compensation therefore.

Section 22. Elections to Be Free

All elections shall be free; and there shall be no hindrance or impediment to the right of a qualified voter to exercise the elective franchise.

Section 23. Capital Cases; Right of Direct Appeal; Effect; Other Cases; Right of Appeal

In all capital cases, appeal directly to the Supreme Court shall be as a matter of right and shall operate as a supersedeas to stay the execution of the sentence of death until further order of the Supreme Court. In all other cases, criminal or civil, an aggrieved party shall be entitled to one appeal to the appellate court created pursuant to Article V, section 1, of this Constitution or to the Supreme Court as may be provided by law.

Section 24. Capital Cases; Right of Direct Appeal; Effect; Other Cases; Right of Appeal

Repealed.

Section 25. Rights of Property; No Discrimination; Aliens

There shall be no discrimination between citizens of the United States in respect to the acquisition, ownership, possession, enjoyment or descent of property. The right of aliens in respect to the acquisition, enjoyment and descent of property may be regulated by law.

Section 26. Powers Retained by People

This enumeration of rights shall not be construed to impair or deny others, retained by the people, and all powers not herein delegated, remain with the people.

Section 27. English Language to Be Official

The English language is hereby declared to be the official language of this state, and all official proceedings, records and publications shall be in such language, and the common school branches shall be taught in said language in public, private, denominational and parochial schools.

Section 28. Crime Victims; Rights Enumerated; Effect; Legislature; Duties

(1) A victim of a crime, as shall be defined by law, or his or her guardian or representative shall have: The right to be informed of all criminal court proceedings; the right to be present at trial unless the trial court finds sequestration necessary for a fair trial for the defendant; and the right to be informed of, be present at, and make an oral or written statement at sentencing, parole, pardon, commutation, and conditional release proceedings. This enumeration of certain rights for crime victims shall not be construed to impair or deny others provided by law or retained by crime victims.

(2) The Legislature shall provide by law for the implementation of the rights granted in this section. There shall be no remedies other than as specifically provided by the Legislature for the enforcement of the rights granted by this section.

(3) Nothing in this section shall constitute a basis for error in favor of a defendant in any criminal proceeding, a basis for providing standing to participate as a party to any criminal proceeding, or a basis to contest the disposition of any charge. Amendments

Section 29. Marriage; Same-Sex Relationships Not Valid or Recognized

Only marriage between a man and a woman shall be valid or recognized in Nebraska. The uniting of two persons of the same sex in a civil union, domestic partnership, or other similar same-sex relationship shall not be valid or recognized in Nebraska.

Section 30. Discrimination or Grant of Preferential Treatment Prohibited; Public Employment, Public Education, or Public Contracting; Section, How Construed; Remedies

(1) The state shall not discriminate against, or grant preferential treatment to, any individual or group on the basis of race, sex, color, ethnicity, or national origin in the operation of public employment, public education, or public contracting.

(2) This section shall apply only to action taken after the section's effective date.

(3) Nothing in this section prohibits bona fide qualifications based on sex that are reasonably necessary to the normal operation of public employment, public education, or public contracting.

(4) Nothing in this section shall invalidate any court order or consent decree that is in force as of the effective date of this section.

(5) Nothing in this section prohibits action that must be taken to establish or maintain eligibility for any federal program, if ineligibility would result in a loss of federal funds to the state.

(6) For purposes of this section, state shall include, but not be limited to:

(a) the State of Nebraska;

(b) any agency, department, office, board, commission, committee, division, unit, branch, bureau, council, or sub-unit of the state;

(c) any public institution of higher education;

(d) any political subdivision of or within the state; and

(e) any government institution or instrumentally of or within the state.

(7) The remedies available for violations of this section shall be the same, regardless of the injured party's race, sex, color, ethnicity, or national origin, as are otherwise available for violations of Nebraska's antidiscrimination law.

(8) This section shall be self executing. If any part or parts of this section are found to be in conflict with federal law or the Constitution of the United States, this section shall be implemented to the maximum extent that federal law and the Constitution of the United States permit. Any provision held invalid shall be severable from the remaining portions of this section.

Article II: Distribution of Powers

Section 1: Legislative, Executive, Judicial

(1) The powers of the government of this state are divided into three distinct departments, the legislative, executive, and judicial, and no person or collection of persons being one of these departments shall exercise any power properly belonging to either of the others except as expressly directed or permitted in this Constitution.

(2) Notwithstanding the provisions of subsection (1) of this section, supervision of individuals sentenced to probation, released on parole, or enrolled in programs or services established within a court may be undertaken by either the judicial or executive department, or jointly, as provided by the Legislature.

Article III: Legislative

Section 1. Legislative Authority; How Vested; Power of Initiative; Power of Referendum

The legislative authority of the state shall be vested in a Legislature consisting of one chamber. The people reserve for themselves the power to propose laws and amendments to the Constitution and to enact or reject the same at the polls, independent of the Legislature, which power shall be called the power of initiative. The people also reserve power at their own option to approve or reject at the polls any act, item, section, or part of any act passed by the Legislature, which power shall be called the power of referendum.

Section 2. First Power Reserved; Initiative

The first power reserved by the people is the initiative whereby laws may be enacted and constitutional amendments adopted by the people independently of the Legislature. This power may be invoked by petition wherein the proposed measure shall be set forth at length. If the petition be for the enactment of a law, it shall be signed by seven percent of the registered voters of the state, and if the petition be for the amendment of the Constitution, the petition therefore shall be signed by ten percent of such registered voters. In all cases the registered voters signing such petition shall be so distributed as to include five percent of the registered voters of each of two-fifths of the counties of the state, and when thus signed, the petition shall be filed with the Secretary of State who shall submit the measure thus proposed to the electors of the state at the first general election held not less than four months after such petition shall have been filed. The same measure, either in form or in essential substance, shall not be submitted to the people by initiative petition, either affirmatively or negatively, more often than once in three years. If conflicting measures submitted to the people at the same election be approved, the one receiving the highest number of affirmative votes shall thereby become law as to all conflicting provisions. The constitutional limitations as to the scope and subject matter of statutes enacted by the Legislature shall apply to those enacted by the initiative. Initiative measures shall contain only one subject. The Legislature shall not amend, repeal, modify, or impair a law enacted by the people by initiative, contemporaneously with the adoption of this initiative measure or at any time thereafter, except upon a vote of at least two-thirds of all the members of the Legislature.

The part of Section 2 which refers to registered voters repeals the reference in Section 4 below which refers to those voting in the preceding gubernatorial election. As per Section 2 above, the number of signatures required for placement of an initiative petition on the ballot by the Nebraska Constitution is equal to 10 percent of the number of registered voters on the date the signatures are to be turned in.

Section 3. Second Power Reserved; Referendum

The second power reserved is the referendum which may be invoked, by petition, against any act or part of an act of the Legislature, except those making appropriations for the expense of the state government or a state institution existing at the time of the passage of such act. Petitions invoking the referendum shall be signed by not less than five percent of the registered voters of the state, distributed as required for initiative petitions, and filed in the office of the Secretary of State within ninety days after the Legislature at which the act sought to be referred was passed shall have adjourned sine die or for more than ninety days. Each such petition shall set out the title of the act against which the referendum is invoked and, in addition thereto, when only a portion of the act is sought to be referred, the number of the section or sections or portion of sections of the act designating such portion. No more than one act or portion of an act of the Legislature shall be the subject of each referendum petition. When the referendum is thus invoked, the Secretary of State shall refer the same to the electors for approval or rejection at the first general election to be held not less than thirty days after the filing of such petition.

When the referendum is invoked as to any act or part of act, other than emergency acts or those for the immediate preservation of the public peace, health, or safety, by petition signed by not less than ten percent of the registered voters of the state distributed as aforesaid, it shall suspend the taking effect of such act or part of act until the same has been approved by the electors of the state.

Section 4. Initiative or Referendum; Signatures Required; Veto; Election Returns; Constitutional Amendments; Non-Partisan Ballot

The whole number of votes cast for Governor at the general election next preceding the filing of an initiative or referendum petition shall be the basis on which the number of signatures to such petition shall be computed. The veto power of the Governor shall not extend to measures initiated by or referred to the people. A measure initiated shall become a law or part of the Constitution, as the case may be, when a majority of the votes cast thereon, and not less than thirty-five per cent of the total vote cast at the election at which the same was submitted, are cast in favor thereof, and shall take effect upon proclamation by the Governor which shall be made within ten days after the official canvass of such votes. The vote upon initiative and referendum measures shall be returned and canvassed in the manner prescribed for the canvass of votes for president. The method of submitting and adopting amendments to the Constitution provided by this section shall be supplementary to the method prescribed in the article of this Constitution, entitled, "Amendments" and the latter shall in no case be construed to conflict herewith. The provisions with respect to the initiative and referendum shall be self-executing, but legislation may be enacted to facilitate their operation. All propositions submitted in pursuance hereof shall be submitted in a nonpartisan manner and without any indication or suggestion on the ballot that they have been approved or endorsed by any political party or organization. Only the title or proper descriptive words of measures shall be printed on the ballot and when two or more measures have the same title they shall be numbered consecutively in the order of filing with the Secretary of State and the number shall be followed by the name of the first petitioner on the corresponding petition.

Section 5. Legislative Districts; Apportionment; Redistricting, When Required

The Legislature shall by law determine the number of members to be elected and divide the state into legislative districts. In the creation of such districts, any county that contains population sufficient to entitle it to two or more members of the Legislature shall be divided into separate and distinct legislative districts, as nearly equal in population as may be and composed of contiguous and compact territory. One member of the Legislature shall be elected from each such district. The basis of apportionment shall be the population excluding aliens, as shown by the next preceding federal census. The Legislature shall redistrict the state after each federal decennial census. In any such redistricting, county lines shall be followed whenever practicable, but other established lines may be followed at the discretion of the Legislature.

Section 6. Legislature; Number of Members; Annual Sessions

The Legislature shall consist of not more than fifty members and not less than thirty members. The sessions of the Legislature shall be annual except as otherwise provided by this constitution or as may be otherwise provided by law.

Section 7. Legislators; Terms; Effect of Redistricting; Election; Salary; Expenses; Mileage

At the general election to be held in November 1964, one-half the members of the Legislature, or as nearly thereto as may be practicable, shall be elected for a term of four years and the remainder for a term of two years, and thereafter all members shall be elected for a term of four years, with the manner of such election to be determined by the Legislature. When the Legislature is redistricted, the members elected prior to the redistricting shall continue in office, and the law providing for such redistricting shall where necessary specify the newly established district which they shall represent for the balance of their term. Each member shall be nominated and elected in a nonpartisan manner and without any indication on the ballot that he or she is affiliated with or endorsed by any political party or organization. Each member of the Legislature shall receive a salary of not to exceed one thousand dollars per month during the term of his or her office. In addition to his or her salary, each member shall receive an amount equal to his or her actual expenses in traveling by the most usual route once to and returning from each regular or special session of the Legislature. Members of the Legislature shall receive no pay nor perquisites other than his or her salary and expenses, and employees of the Legislature shall receive no compensation other than their salary or per diem.

Section 8. Legislators; Qualifications; One-Year Residence in District; Removal from District, Effect

No person shall be eligible to the office of member of the Legislature unless on the date of the general election at which he is elected, or on the date of his appointment he is a registered voter, has attained the age of twenty-one years and has resided within the district from which he is elected for the term of one year next before his election, unless he shall have been absent on the public business of the United States or of this State. And no person elected as aforesaid shall hold his office after he shall have removed from such district.

Section 9. Legislators; Disqualifications; Election to Other Office; Resignation Required

No person holding office under the authority of the United States, or any lucrative office under the authority of this state, shall be eligible to or have a seat in the Legislature. No person elected or appointed to the Legislature shall receive any civil appointment to a state office while holding membership in the Legislature or while the Legislature is in session, and all such appointments shall be void. Except as otherwise provided by law, a member of the Legislature who is elected to any other state or local office prior to the end of his or her term in the Legislature shall resign from the Legislature prior to the commencement of the legislative session during which the term of the state or local office will begin.

Section 10. Legislative Sessions; Time; Quorum; Rules of Procedure; Expulsion of Members; Disrespectful Behavior, Penalty

Beginning with the year 1975, regular sessions of the Legislature shall be held annually, commencing at 10 a.m. on the first Wednesday after the first Monday in January of each year. The duration of regular sessions held shall not exceed ninety legislative days in odd-numbered years unless extended by a vote of four-fifths of all members elected to the Legislature, and shall not exceed sixty legislative days in even-numbered years unless extended by a vote of four-fifths of all members elected to the Legislature. Bills and resolutions under consideration by the Legislature upon adjournment of a regular session held in an odd-numbered year may be considered at the next regular session, as if there had been no such adjournment. The Lieutenant Governor shall preside, but shall vote only when the Legislature is equally divided. A majority of the members elected to the Legislature shall constitute a quorum; the Legislature shall determine the rules of its proceedings and be the judge of the election, returns, and qualifications of its members, shall choose its own officers, including a Speaker to preside when the

Lieutenant Governor shall be absent, incapacitated, or shall act as Governor. No member shall be expelled except by a vote of two-thirds of all members elected to the Legislature, and no member shall be twice expelled for the same offense. The Legislature may punish by imprisonment any person not a member thereof who shall be guilty of disrespect to the Legislature by disorderly or contemptuous behavior in its presence, but no such imprisonment shall extend beyond twenty-four hours at one time, unless the person shall persist in such disorderly or contemptuous behavior.

Section 11. Legislative Journal; Vote Viva Voce; Open Doors; Committee Votes

The Legislature shall keep a journal of its proceedings and publish them, except such parts as may require secrecy, and the yeas and nays of the members on any question shall at the desire of any one of them be entered on the journal. All votes shall be viva voce. The doors of the Legislature and of the committees of the Legislature shall be open, except when the business shall be such as ought to be kept secret. The yeas and nays of each member of any committee of the Legislature shall be recorded and published on any question in committee to advance or to indefinitely postpone any bill.

Section 12. Legislators; Terms; Limitation

(1) No person shall be eligible to serve as a member of the Legislature for four years next after the expiration of two consecutive terms regardless of the district represented.

(2) Service prior to January 1, 2001, as a member of the Legislature shall not be counted for the purpose of calculating consecutive terms in subsection (1) of this section.

(3) For the purpose of this section, service in office for more than one-half of a term shall be deemed service for a term.

Section 13. Style of Bills; Majority Necessary to Passage; Yeas and Nays Entered on Journal

The style of all bills shall be, Be it enacted by the people of the State of Nebraska, and no law shall be enacted except by bill. No bill shall be passed by the Legislature unless by the assent of a majority of all members elected and the yeas and nays on the question of final passage of any bill shall be entered upon the journal.

Section 14. Bills and Resolutions Read by Title; Printing; Vote for Final Passage; Bills to Contain One Subject; Amended Section to Be Set Forth; Signing of Bills

Every bill and resolution shall be read by title when introduced, and a printed copy thereof provided for the use of each member. The bill and all amendments thereto shall be printed and presented before the vote is taken upon its final passage and shall be read at large unless three-fifths of all the members elected to the Legislature vote not to read the bill and all amendments at large. No vote upon the final passage of any bill shall be taken until five legislative days after its introduction nor until it has been on file for final reading and passage for at least one legislative day. No bill shall contain more than one subject, and the subject shall be clearly expressed in the title. No law shall be amended unless the new act contains the section or sections as amended and the section or sections so amended shall be repealed. The Lieutenant Governor, or the Speaker if acting as presiding officer, shall sign, in the presence of the Legislature while it is in session and capable of transacting business, all bills and resolutions passed by the Legislature.

Section 15. Members Privileged from Arrest

Members of the Legislature in all cases except treason, felony or breach of the peace, shall be privileged from arrest during the session of the Legislature, and for fifteen days next before the commencement and after the termination thereof.

Section 16. Members of the Legislature and State Officers; Conflicts of Interest; Standards for

No member of the Legislature or any state officer shall have a conflict of interest, as defined by the Legislature, directly in any contract, with the state or any county or municipality thereof, authorized by any law enacted during the term for which he shall have been elected or appointed, or within one year after the expiration of such term. The Legislature shall prescribe standards and definitions for determining the existence of such conflicts of interest in contracts, and it shall prescribe sanctions for enforcing this section.

Section 17. Impeachment; Procedure

The Legislature shall have the sole power of impeachment, but a majority of the members elected must concur therein. Proceedings may be initiated in either a regular session or a special session of the Legislature. Upon the adoption of a resolution of impeachment, which resolution shall give reasonable notice of the acts or omissions alleged to constitute impeachable offenses but need not conform to any particular style, a notice of an impeachment of any officer, other than a Judge of the Supreme Court, shall be forthwith served upon the Chief Justice, by the Clerk of the Legislature, who shall thereupon call a session of the Supreme Court to meet at the Capitol in an expeditious fashion after such notice to try the impeachment. A notice of an impeachment of the Chief Justice or any Judge of the Supreme Court shall be served by the Clerk of the Legislature, upon the clerk of the judicial district within which the Capitol is located, and he or she thereupon shall choose, at random, seven Judges of the District Court in the State to meet within thirty days at the Capitol, to sit as a Court to try such impeachment, which Court shall organize by electing one of its number to preside. The case against the impeached civil officer shall be brought in the name of the Legislature and shall be managed by two senators, appointed by the Legislature, who may make technical or procedural amendments to the articles of impeachment as they deem necessary. The trial shall be conducted in the manner of a civil proceeding and the impeached civil officer shall not be allowed to invoke a privilege against self-incrimination, except as otherwise applicable in a general civil case. No person shall be convicted without the concurrence of two-thirds of the members of the Court of impeachment that clear and convincing evidence exists indicating that such person is guilty of one or more impeachable offenses, but judgment in cases of impeachment shall not extend further than removal from office and disqualification to hold and enjoy any office of honor, profit, or trust, in this State, but the party impeached, whether convicted or acquitted, shall nevertheless be liable to prosecution and punishment according to law. No officer shall exercise his or her official duties after he or she shall have been impeached and notified thereof, until he or she shall have been acquitted.

Section 18. Local or Special Laws Prohibited

The Legislature shall not pass local or special laws in any of the following cases, that is to say:

For granting divorces.

Changing the names of persons or places.

Laying out, opening altering and working roads or highways.

Vacating roads, Town plats, streets, alleys, and public grounds.

Locating or changing County seats.

Regulating County and Township offices.

Regulating the practice of Courts of Justice.

Regulating the jurisdiction and duties of Justices of the Peace, Police Magistrates and Constables.

Providing for changes of venue in civil and criminal cases.

Incorporating Cities, Towns and Villages, or changing or amending the charter of any Town, City, or Village.

Providing for the election of Officers in Townships, incorporated Towns or Cities.

Summoning or empaneling Grand or Petit Juries.
Providing for the bonding of cities, towns, precincts, school districts or other municipalities.

Providing for the management of Public Schools.
The opening and conducting of any election, or designating the place of voting.

The sale or mortgage of real estate belonging to minors, or others under disability.

The protection of game or fish.

Chartering or licensing ferries, or toll bridges, remitting fines, penalties or forfeitures, creating, increasing and decreasing fees, percentage or allowances of public officers, during the term for which said officers are elected or appointed.

Changing the law of descent.

Granting to any corporation, association, or individual, the right to lay down railroad tracks, or amending existing charters for such purpose.

Granting to any corporation, association, or individual any special or exclusive privileges, immunity, or franchise whatever; PROVIDED, that notwithstanding any other provisions of this Constitution, the Legislature shall have authority to separately define and classify loans and installment sales, to establish maximum rates within classifications of loans or installment sales which it establishes, and to regulate with respect thereto. In all other cases where a general law can be made applicable, no special law shall be enacted.

Section 19. Compensation; Increase When; Extra Compensation to Public Officers and Contractors Prohibited; Retirement Benefits; Adjustment

The Legislature shall never grant any extra compensation to any public officer, agent, or servant after the services have been rendered nor to any contractor after the contract has been entered into, except that retirement benefits of retired public officers and employees may be adjusted to reflect changes in the cost of living and wage levels that have occurred subsequent to the date of retirement.

The compensation of any public officer, including any officer whose compensation is fixed by the Legislature, shall not be increased or diminished during his or her term of office, except that when there are members elected or appointed to the Legislature or the judiciary, or officers elected or appointed to a board or commission having more than one member, and the terms of such members commence and end at different times, the compensation of all members of the Legislature, of the judiciary, or of such board or commission may be increased or diminished at the beginning of the full term of any member thereof.

Nothing in this section shall prevent local governing bodies from reviewing and adjusting vested pension benefits periodically as prescribed by ordinance.

The surviving spouse of any retired public officer, agent, or servant, who has retired under a pension plan or system, shall be considered as having pensionable status and shall be entitled to the same benefits which may, at any time, be provided for or available to spouses of other public officers, agents, or servants who have retired under such pension plan or system at a later date, and such benefits shall not be prohibited by the restrictions of this section or of Article XIII, section 3 of the Constitution of Nebraska.

Section 20. Salt Springs, Coal, Oil, Minerals; Alienation Prohibited

The salt springs, coal, oil, minerals, or other natural resources on or contained in the land belonging to the state shall never be alienated; but provision may be made by law for the leasing or development of the same.

Section 21. Donation of State Lands Prohibited; When

Lands under control of the State shall never be donated to railroad companies, private corporations or individuals.

Section 22. Appropriations for State; Deficiencies; Bills for Pay of Members and Officials

Each Legislature shall make appropriations for the expenses of the Government. And whenever it is deemed necessary to make further appropriations for deficiencies, the same shall require a two-thirds vote of all the members elected to the Legislature. Bills making appropriations for the pay of members and officers of the Legislature, and for the salaries of the officers of the Government, shall contain no provision on any other subject.

Section 23. Repealed.

Section 24. Games of Chance, Lotteries, and Gift Enterprises; Restrictions; Parimutuel Wagering on Horseraces; Bingo Games; Use of State Lottery Proceeds

(1) Except as provided in this section, the Legislature shall not authorize any game of chance or any lottery or gift enterprise when the consideration for a chance to participate involves the payment of money for the purchase of property, services, or a chance or admission ticket or requires an expenditure of substantial effort or time.

(2) The Legislature may authorize and regulate a state lottery pursuant to subsection (3) of this section and other lotteries, raffles, and gift enterprises which are intended solely as business promotions or the proceeds of which are to be used solely for charitable or community betterment purposes without profit to the promoter of such lotteries, raffles, or gift enterprises.

(3) (a) The Legislature may establish a lottery to be operated and regulated by the State of Nebraska. The proceeds of the lottery shall be appropriated by the Legislature for the costs of establishing and maintaining the lottery and for the following purposes, as directed by the Legislature:

(i) The first five hundred thousand dollars after the payment of prizes and operating expenses shall be transferred to the Compulsive Gamblers Assistance Fund;

(ii) Forty-four and one-half percent of the money remaining after the payment of prizes and operating expenses and the initial transfer to the Compulsive Gamblers Assistance Fund shall be transferred to the Nebraska Environmental Trust Fund to be used as provided in the Nebraska Environmental Trust Act;

(iii) Forty-four and one-half percent of the money remaining after the payment of prizes and operating expenses and the initial transfer to the Compulsive Gamblers Assistance Fund shall be used for education as the Legislature may direct;

(iv) Ten percent of the money remaining after the payment of prizes and operating expenses and the initial transfer to the Compulsive Gamblers Assistance Fund shall be transferred to the Nebraska State Fair Board if the most populous city within the county in which the fair is located provides matching funds equivalent to ten percent of the funds available for transfer. Such matching funds may be obtained from the city and any other private or public entity, except that no portion of such matching funds shall be provided by the state. If the Nebraska State Fair ceases operations, ten percent of the money remaining after the payment of prizes and operating expenses and the initial transfer to the Compulsive Gamblers Assistance Fund shall be transferred to the General Fund; and

(v) One percent of the money remaining after the payment of prizes and operating expenses and the initial transfer to the Compulsive Gamblers Assistance Fund shall be transferred to the Compulsive Gamblers Assistance Fund.

(b) No lottery game shall be conducted as part of the lottery unless the type of game has been approved by a majority of the members of the Legislature.

(4) Nothing in this section shall be construed to prohibit

(a) the enactment of laws providing for the licensing and regulation of wagering on the results of horseraces, wherever run, either within or outside of the state, by the parimutuel method, when such wagering is conducted by licensees within a licensed racetrack enclosure or

(b) the enactment of laws providing for the licensing and regulation of bingo games conducted by nonprofit associations which have been in existence for a period of five years immediately preceding the application for license, except that bingo games cannot be conducted by agents or lessees of such associations on a percentage basis.

Section 25. Incidental Expenses of State Officers; Specific Appropriations Always Necessary; Warrants for Money

No allowance shall be made for the incidental expenses of any state officer except the same be made by general appropriation and upon an account specifying each item. No money shall be drawn from the treasury except in pursuance of a specific appropriation made by law, and on the presentation of a warrant issued as the Legislature may direct, and no money shall be diverted from any appropriation made for any purpose or taken from any fund whatever by resolution.

Section 26. Privilege of Members

No member of the Legislature shall be liable in any civil or criminal action whatever for words spoken in debate.

Section 27. Acts Take Effect After Three Months; Emergency Bills; Session Laws

No act shall take effect until three calendar months after the adjournment of the session at which it passed, unless in case of emergency, which is expressed in the preamble or body of the act, the Legislature shall by a vote of two-thirds of all the members elected otherwise direct. All laws shall be published within sixty days after the adjournment of each session and distributed among the several counties in such manner as the Legislature may provide.

Section 28. Repealed.

Section 29. Legislative Authority in Emergencies Due to Enemy Attack upon United States

(1). In order to insure continuity of state and local governmental operations in periods of emergency resulting from enemy attack upon the United States, or the imminent threat thereof, the

Legislature shall have the power and the immediate duty, notwithstanding any other provision to the contrary in this Constitution, to provide by law for:

(a) The prompt and temporary succession to the powers and duties of all public offices, of whatever nature and whether filled by election or appointment, the incumbents of which, after an attack, may be or become unavailable or unable to carry on the powers and duties of such offices;

(b) The convening of the Legislature into general or extraordinary session, upon or without call by the Governor, during or after a war or enemy caused disaster occurring in the United States; and, with respect to any such emergency session, the suspension or temporary change of the provisions of this Constitution or of general law relating to the length and purposes of any legislative session or prescribing the specific proportion or number of legislators whose presence or vote is necessary to constitute a quorum or to accomplish any legislative act or function;

(c) The selection and changing from time to time of a temporary state seat of government, of temporary county seats, and of temporary seats of government for other political subdivisions; to be used if made necessary by enemy attack or imminent threat thereof;

(d) The determination, selection, reproduction, preservation, and dispersal of public records necessary to the continuity of governmental operations in the event of enemy attack or imminent threat thereof; and

(e) Such other measures and procedures as may be necessary and proper for insuring the continuity of governmental operations in the event of enemy attack or imminent threat thereof.

(2). In the exercise of the powers hereinbefore conferred, the Legislature shall in all respects conform to the requirements of this Constitution except to the extent that, in the judgment of the Legislature, so to do would be impracticable or would admit of undue delay.

Section 30. Legislature to Pass Necessary Laws

The Legislature shall pass all laws necessary to carry into effect the provisions of this constitution.

Article IV: Executive

Section 1. Executive Departments; officers; When Elected; Terms; Eligibility; Books to Be Kept at Seat of Government; Residence of Officers; Heads of Departments; Appointments

The executive officers of the state shall be the Governor, Lieutenant Governor, Secretary of State, Auditor of Public Accounts, State Treasurer, Attorney General, and the heads of such other executive departments as set forth herein or as may be established by law. The Legislature may provide for the placing of the above named officers as heads over such departments of government as it may by law establish.
The Governor, Lieutenant Governor, Attorney General, Secretary of State, Auditor of Public Accounts, and State Treasurer shall be chosen at the general election held in November 1974, and in each alternate even-numbered year thereafter, for a term of four years and until their successors shall be elected and qualified. Each candidate for Governor shall select a person to be the candidate for Lieutenant Governor on the general election ballot. In the general election one vote shall be cast jointly for the candidates for Governor and Lieutenant Governor. The Governor shall be ineligible to the office of Governor for four years next after the expiration of two consecutive terms for which he or she was elected.

The records, books, and papers of all executive officers shall be kept at the seat of government. Executive officers shall reside within the State of Nebraska during their respective terms of office. Officers in the executive department of the state shall perform such duties as may be provided by law.
The heads of all executive departments established by law, other than those to be elected as provided herein, shall be appointed by the Governor, with the consent of a majority of all members elected to the Legislature, but officers so appointed may be removed by the Governor. Subject to the provisions of this Constitution, the heads of the various executive or civil

departments shall have power to appoint and remove all subordinate employees in their respective departments.

Section 2. Governor; Lieutenant Governor; Eligibility; Qualifications; Appointive Officers, Ineligible for Other Office

No person shall be eligible to the office of Governor, or Lieutenant Governor, who shall not have attained the age of thirty years, and who shall not have been for five years next preceding his election a resident and citizen of this state and a citizen of the United States. None of the appointive officers mentioned in this article shall be eligible to any other state office during the period for which they have been appointed.

Section 3. Treasurer; Ineligibility

The treasurer shall be ineligible to the office of treasurer, for two years next after the expiration of two consecutive terms for which he was elected.

Section 4. Election Returns; Canvass by Legislature; Conduct of Election Contests

The returns of every election for the officers of the executive department shall be sealed up and transmitted by the returning officers to the Secretary of State, directed to the Speaker of the Legislature, who shall immediately after the organization of the Legislature, and before proceeding to other business, open and publish the same in the presence of a majority of the members of the Legislature. The person having the highest number of votes for each of said offices shall be declared duly elected; but if two or more have an equal and the highest number of votes, the Legislature shall choose one of such persons for said office. The conduct of election contests for any of said offices shall be in such manner as may be prescribed by law.

Section 5. Impeachment

All civil officers of this state shall be liable to impeachment for any misdemeanor in office.

Section 6. Supreme Executive Power

The supreme executive power shall be vested in the Governor, who shall take care that the laws be faithfully executed and the affairs of the state efficiently and economically administered.

Section 7. Message by Governor; Budget; Contents; Budget Bill; Preparation; Appropriations Not to Be in Excess of Budget; Exception; Excess Subject to Veto

The Governor may, at the commencement of each session, and at the close of his term of office and whenever the Legislature may require, give by message to the Legislature information of the condition of the state, and shall recommend such measures as he shall deem expedient. At a time fixed by law, he shall present, by message, a complete itemized budget of the financial requirements of all departments, institutions and agencies of the state and a budget bill to be introduced by the Speaker of the Legislature at the request of the Governor. Said budget bill shall be prepared with such expert assistance and under such regulations as may be required by the Governor. No appropriations shall be made in excess of the recommendation contained in such budget including any amendment the Governor may make thereto unless by three-fifths vote of the Legislature, and such excess so approved shall be subject to veto by the Governor.

Section 8. Special Sessions

The Governor may, on extraordinary occasions, convene the Legislature by proclamation, stating therein the purpose for which they are convened, and the Legislature shall enter upon no business except that for which they were called together.

Section 9. Repealed.

Section 10. Governor to Appoint Officers; Removal

The Governor shall appoint with the approval of a majority of the Legislature, all persons whose offices are established by the Constitution, or which may be created by law, and whose appointment or election is not otherwise by law or herein provided for; and no such person shall be appointed or elected by the Legislature. The Governor shall have power to remove, for cause and after a public hearing, any person whom he may appoint for a term except officers provided for in Article V of the Constitution, and he may declare his office vacant, and fill the same as herein provided as in other cases of vacancy. The Governor shall have power to remove any other person whom he appoints at any time and for any reason.

Section 11. Elected State Officer; Vacation of Office; Governor Fill by Appointment; Term

If any elected state office created by this Constitution, except offices provided for in Article V of this Constitution, shall be vacated by death, resignation or otherwise, it shall be the duty of the Governor to fill that office by appointment, and the appointee shall hold the office until his successor shall be elected and qualified in such manner as may be provided by law.

Section 12. Nonelective State Officers; Vacation; Governor; Fill the Office by Appointment; Approval by Legislature

If any nonelective state office, except offices provided for in Article V of this Constitution, shall be vacated by death, resignation or otherwise, it shall be the duty of the Governor to fill that office by appointment. If the Legislature is in session, such appointment shall be subject to the approval of a majority of the members of the Legislature. If the Legislature is not in session, the Governor shall make a temporary appointment until the next session of the Legislature, at which time a majority of the members of the Legislature shall have the right to approve or disapprove the appointment. All appointees shall hold their office until their successors shall be appointed and qualified. No person after being rejected by the Legislature shall be again nominated for the same office at the same session, unless at request of the Legislature, or be appointed to the same office during the recess or adjournment of the Legislature.

Section 13. Board of Parole; Members; Powers; Reprieves; Proceedings; Power to Pardon; Limitations

The Legislature shall provide by law for the establishment of a Board of Parole and the qualifications of its members. Said board, or a majority thereof, shall have power to grant paroles after conviction and judgment, under such conditions as may be prescribed by law, for any offenses committed against the criminal laws of this state except treason and cases of impeachment. The Governor, Attorney General and Secretary of State, sitting as a board, shall have power to remit fines and forfeitures and to grant respites, reprieves, pardons, or commutations in all cases of conviction for offenses against the laws of the state, except treason and cases of impeachment. The Board of Parole may advise the Governor, Attorney General and Secretary of State on the merits of any application for remission, respite, reprieve, pardon or commutation but such advice shall not be binding on them. The Governor shall have power to suspend the execution of the sentence imposed for treason until the case can be reported to the Legislature at its next session, when the Legislature shall either grant a pardon, or commute the sentence or direct the execution, or grant a further reprieve.

Section 14. Governor to Be Commander-in-Chief of Militia

The Governor shall be commander-in-chief of the military and naval forces of the state (except when they shall be called into the service of the United States) and may call out the same to execute the laws, suppress insurrection, and repel invasion.

Section 15. Bills to Be Presented to Governor; Approval; Procedure; Disapproval or Reduction of Items of Appropriation; Passage Despite Disapproval or Reduction

Every bill passed by the Legislature, before it becomes a law, shall be presented to the Governor. If he approves he shall sign it, and thereupon it shall become a law, but if he does not approve or reduces any item or items of appropriations, he shall return it with his objections to the Legislature, which shall enter the objections at large upon its journal, and proceed to reconsider the bill with the objections as a whole, or proceed to reconsider individually the item or items disapproved or reduced. If then three-fifths of the members elected agree to pass the bill with objections it shall become a law, or if three-fifths of the members elected agree to repass any item or items disapproved or reduced, the bill with such repassage shall become a law. In all cases the vote shall be determined by yeas and nays, to be entered upon the journal. Any bill which shall not be returned by the Governor within five days (Sundays excepted) after it shall have been presented to him, shall become a law in like manner as if he had signed it; unless the Legislature by their adjournment prevent its return; in which case it shall be filed, with his objections, in the office of the Secretary of State within five days after such adjournment, or become a law. The Governor may disapprove or reduce any item or items of appropriation contained in bills passed by the Legislature, and the item or items so disapproved shall be stricken therefrom, and the items reduced shall remain as reduced unless the Legislature has reconsidered the item or items disapproved or reduced and has repassed any such item or items over the objection of the Governor by a three-fifths approval of the members elected.

Section 16. Order of Succession to Become Governor; Lieutenant Governor; Duties

In case of the conviction of the Governor on impeachment, his removal from office, his resignation or his death, the Lieutenant Governor, the Speaker of the Legislature and such other persons designated by law shall in that order be Governor for the remainder of the Governor's term.

In case of the death of the Governor-elect, the Lieutenant Governor-elect, the Speaker of the Legislature and such other persons designated by law shall become Governor in that order at the commencement of the Governor-elect's term.

If the Governor or the person in line of succession to serve as Governor is absent from the state, or suffering under an inability, the powers and duties of the office of Governor shall devolve in order of precedence until the absence or inability giving rise to the devolution of powers ceases as provided by law. After January 1, 1975, the Lieutenant Governor shall serve on all boards and commissions in lieu of the Governor whenever so designated by the Governor, shall perform such duties as may be delegated him by the Governor, and shall devote his full time to the duties of his office.

Section 17. Repealed.

Section 18. Repealed.

Section 19. State Institutions; Management, Control, and Government; Determination by Legislature

The general management, control and government of all state charitable, mental, reformatory, and penal institutions shall be vested as determined by the Legislature.

Section 20.

Public Service Commission; Membership; Terms; Powers

There shall be a Public Service Commission, consisting of not less than three nor more than seven members, as the Legislature shall prescribe, whose term of office shall be six years, and whose compensation shall be fixed by the Legislature. Commissioners shall be elected by districts of substantially equal population as the Legislature shall provide. The powers and duties of such commission shall include the regulation of rates, service and general control of common carriers as the Legislature may provide by law. But, in the absence of specific legislation, the commission shall exercise the powers and perform the duties enumerated in this provision.

Section 21. Repealed.

Section 22. Executive Officials to Keep Accounts; Reports; False Reports, Penalty

The Legislature shall provide by statute for the keeping of accounts and the reporting by those agencies of the state which are required to administer cash funds not subject to appropriation by the Legislature, and an annual report thereof shall be made to the Governor under oath; and any officer who makes a false report shall be guilty of perjury and punished accordingly.

Section 23. Executive Officials and Heads of Institutions; Reports to Legislature; Information from Expending Agencies

All expending agencies of the state as the Legislature may provide shall at least ten days preceding each regular session of the Legislature severally report to the Governor, who shall transmit such reports to the Legislature, together with the reports of the Judges of the Supreme Court of defects in the constitution and laws, and the Governor or the Legislature may at any time require information, in writing, under oath, from the officers of all expending agencies, upon any subject relating to the condition, management and expenses of their respective offices.

Section 24. Great Seal

There shall be a seal of the state, which shall be called the "Great Seal of the State of Nebraska," which shall be kept by the Secretary of State and used by him officially as directed by law.

Section 25. Salaries of Officials; Fees

The officers provided for in this article shall receive such salaries as may be provided by law. Such officers, or such other officers as may be provided for by law, shall not receive for their own use any fees, costs, or interest upon public money in their hands. All fees that may hereafter be payable by law for services performed, or received by an officer provided for in this article, by virtue of his office shall be paid forthwith into the state treasury.

Section 26. Officials to Give Bonds

All officers of government shall give bond as may be prescribed by law.

Section 27. Executive Offices; Creation of

No executive state office other than herein provided shall be created except by a two-thirds majority of all members elected to the Legislature.

Section 28. Tax Equalization and Review Commission; Members; Powers; Tax Commissioner; Powers

By January 1, 1997, there shall be a Tax Equalization and Review Commission. The members of the commission shall be appointed by the Governor as provided by law. The commission shall have power to review and equalize assessments of property for taxation within the state and shall have such other powers and perform such other duties as the Legislature may provide. The terms of office and compensation of members of the commission shall be as provided by law.

A Tax Commissioner shall be appointed by the Governor with the approval of the Legislature. The Tax Commissioner may have jurisdiction over the administration of the revenue laws of the state and such other duties and powers as provided by law. The Tax Commissioner shall serve at the pleasure of the Governor.

Article V: Judicial

Section 1. Power Vested in Courts; Chief Justice; Powers

The judicial power of the state shall be vested in a Supreme Court, an appellate court, district courts, county courts, in and for each county, with one or more judges for each county or with one judge for two or more counties, as the Legislature shall provide, and such other courts inferior to the Supreme Court as may be created by law. In accordance with rules established by the Supreme Court and not in conflict with other provisions of this Constitution and laws governing such matters, general administrative authority over all courts in this state shall be vested in the Supreme Court and shall be exercised by the Chief Justice. The Chief Justice shall be the executive head of the courts and may appoint an administrative director thereof.

Section 2. Supreme Court; Number of Judges; Quorum; Jurisdiction; Retired Judges, Temporary Duty; Court Divisions; Assignments by Chief Justice

The Supreme Court shall consist of seven judges, one of whom shall be the Chief Justice. A majority of the judges shall be necessary to constitute a quorum. A majority of the members sitting shall have authority to pronounce a decision except in cases involving the constitutionality of an act of the Legislature. No legislative act shall be held unconstitutional except by the concurrence of five judges. The Supreme Court shall have jurisdiction in all cases relating to the revenue, civil cases in which the state is a party, mandamus, quo warranto, habeas corpus, election contests involving state officers other than members of the Legislature, and such appellate jurisdiction as may be provided by law. The Legislature may provide that any judge of the Supreme Court or judge of the appellate court created pursuant to Article V, section 1, of this Constitution who has retired may be called upon for temporary duty by the Supreme Court. Whenever necessary for the prompt submission and determination of causes, the Supreme Court may appoint judges of the district court or the appellate court to act as associate judges of the Supreme Court, sufficient in number, with the judges of the Supreme Court, to constitute two divisions of the court of five judges in each division. Whenever judges of the district court or the appellate court are so acting, the court shall sit in two divisions, and four of the judges thereof shall be necessary to constitute a quorum. Judges of the district court or the appellate court so appointed shall serve during the pleasure of the court and shall have all the powers of judges of the Supreme Court. The Chief Justice shall make assignments of judges to the divisions of the court, preside over the division of which he or she is a member, and designate the presiding judge of the other division. The judges of the Supreme Court, sitting without division, shall hear and determine all cases involving the constitutionality of a statute and all appeals involving capital cases and may review any decision rendered by a division of the court. In such cases, in the event of the disability or disqualification by interest or otherwise of any of the judges of the Supreme Court, the court may appoint judges of the district court or the appellate court to sit temporarily as judges of the Supreme Court, sufficient to constitute a full court of seven judges. Judges of the district court or the appellate court shall receive no additional salary by virtue of their appointment and service as herein provided, but they shall be reimbursed their necessary traveling and hotel expenses.

Section 3. Terms of Supreme Court

At least two terms of the supreme court shall be held each year, at the seat of government.

Section 4. Chief Justice and Judges of the Supreme Court; Selection; Residence; Location of Offices

The Chief Justice and the Judges of the Supreme Court shall be selected as provided in this Article V. They may reside at the place where the court is located but shall reside within the state, and no Chief Justice or Judge of the Supreme Court shall be deemed thereby to have lost his or her residence at the place from which he or she was selected. The offices of the Chief Justice and Judges of the Supreme Court shall be at the place where the court is located.

Section 5. Supreme Court Judicial Districts; Redistricting; When

The Legislature shall divide the state into six contiguous and compact districts of approximately equal population, which shall be numbered from one to six, which shall be known as the Supreme Court judicial districts. The Legislature shall redistrict the state after each federal decennial census. In any such redistricting, county lines shall be followed whenever practicable, but other established lines may be followed at the discretion of the Legislature. Such districts shall not be changed except upon the concurrence of a majority of the members of the Legislature. Whenever the Supreme Court is redistricted, the judges serving prior to the redistricting shall continue in office, and the law providing for such redistricting shall where necessary specify the newly established districts which they shall represent for the balance of their terms.

Section 6. Chief Justice to Preside

The Chief Justice shall preside at all terms and sittings of the supreme court, and in his absence or disability the judges present shall select one of their number chief justice pro tempore.

Section 7. Chief Justice; Associate Justices; Qualifications

No person shall be eligible to the office of Chief Justice or Judge of the Supreme Court unless he shall be at least thirty years of age, and a citizen of the United States, and shall have resided in this state at least three years next preceding his selection; nor, in the case of a Judge of the Supreme Court selected from a Supreme Court judicial district, unless he shall be a resident and elector of the district from which selected.

Section 8. Supreme Court Appoint Staff; Budget; Copyright of State Reports

The Supreme Court shall appoint such staff as may be needed for the proper dispatch of the business of the court. The court shall prepare and recommend to each session of the Legislature a budget of the estimated expenses of the court. The copyright of the state reports shall forever remain the property of the state.

Section 9. District Courts; Jurisdiction; Felons May Plead Guilty; Sentence

The district courts shall have both chancery and common law jurisdiction, and such other jurisdiction as the Legislature may provide; and the judges thereof may admit persons charged with felony to a plea of guilty and pass such sentence as may be prescribed by law.

Section 10. District Court Judicial Districts

The state shall be divided into district court judicial districts. Until otherwise provided by law, the boundaries of the judicial districts and the number of judges of the district courts shall remain as now fixed. The judges of the district courts shall be selected from the respective districts as provided in this Article V.

Section 11. District Court Judges; Change of Number; Boundaries

The Legislature may change the number of judges of the district courts and alter the boundaries of judicial districts. Such change in number or alterations in boundaries shall not vacate the office of any judge. Such districts shall be formed of compact territory bounded by county lines.

Section 12. District Court Judges May Hold Court for Each Other; Retired Judges, Temporary duty

The judges of the district court may hold court for each other and shall do so when required by law or when ordered by the Supreme Court. The Legislature may provide that any judge of the district court who has retired may be called upon for temporary duty by the Supreme Court.

Section 13. Supreme and District Judges; Salaries

The chief justice, the judges of the supreme court and the judges of the district court shall receive such salaries as may be provided by law.

Section 14. Supreme and District Judges Not to Act as Attorneys; Judge Not to Practice Law, When

No judge of the Supreme or district courts shall act as attorney or counsellor at law in any manner whatsoever. No judge shall practice law in any court in any matter arising in or growing out of any proceedings in his own court.

Section 15. Repealed.

Section 16. Repealed.

Section 17. Repealed.

Section 18. Repealed.

Section 19. Practice of All Courts to Be Uniform

The organization, jurisdiction, powers, proceedings, and practice of all courts of the same class or grade, so far as regulated by law and the force and effect of the proceedings, judgments and decrees of such courts, severally, shall be uniform.

Section 20. Officers in This Article; Tenure; Residence; Duties; Compensation

All officers provided for in this Article shall hold their offices until their successors shall be qualified and they shall respectively reside in the district or county from which they shall be selected. All officers, when not otherwise provided for in this Article, shall perform such duties and receive such compensation as may be prescribed by law.

Section 21. Merit Plan for Selection of Judges; Terms of Office; Filling of Vacancies; Procedure; Voting for Nominee

(1) In the case of any vacancy in the Supreme Court or in any district court or in such other court or courts made subject to this provision by law, such vacancy shall be filled by the Governor from a list of at least two nominees presented to him by the appropriate judicial nominating commission. If the Governor shall fail to make an appointment from the list within sixty days from the date it is presented to him, the appointment shall be made by the Chief Justice or the acting Chief Justice of the Supreme Court from the same list.

(2) In all other cases, any vacancy shall be filled as provided by law.

(3) At the next general election following the expiration of three years from the date of appointment of any judge under the provisions of subsection (1) of this section and every six years thereafter as long as such judge retains office, each Justice or Judge of the Supreme Court or district court or such other court or courts as the Legislature shall provide shall have his right to remain in office subject to approval or rejection by the electorate in such manner as the Legislature shall provide; Provided, that every judge holding or elected to an office described in subsection (1) of this section on the effective date of this amendment whether by election or appointment, upon qualification shall be deemed to have been selected and to have once received the approval of the electorate as herein provided, and shall be required to submit his right to continue in office to the approval or rejection of the electorate at the general election next preceding the expiration of the term of office for which such judge was elected or appointed, and every six years thereafter. In the case of the Chief Justice of the Supreme Court, the electorate of the entire state shall vote on the question of approval or rejection. In the case of any Judge of the Supreme Court, other than the Chief Justice, and any judge of the district court or any other court made subject to subsection (1) of this section, the electorate of the district from which such judge was selected shall vote on the question of such approval or rejection.

(4) There shall be a judicial nominating commission for the Chief Justice of the Supreme Court and one for each judicial district of the Supreme Court and of the district court and one for each area or district served by any other court made subject to subsection (1) of this section by law. Each judicial nominating commission shall consist of nine members, one of whom shall be a Judge of the Supreme Court who shall be designated by the Governor and shall act as chairman, but shall not be entitled to vote. The members of the bar of the state residing in the area from which the nominees are to be selected shall designate four of their number to serve as members of said commission, and the Governor shall appoint four citizens, not admitted to practice law before the courts of the state, from among the residents of the same geographical area to serve as members of said commission. Not more than four of such voting members shall be of the same political party. The terms of office for members of each judicial nominating commission shall be staggered and shall be fixed by the Legislature. The nominees of any such commission cannot include a member of such commission or any person who has served as a member of such commission within a period of two years immediately preceding his nomination or for such additional period as the Legislature shall provide. The names of candidates shall be released to the public prior to a public hearing.

(5) Members of the nominating commission shall vote for the nominee of their choice by roll call. Each candidate must receive a majority of the voting members of the nominating commission to have his name submitted to the Governor.

Section 22. State May Sue and Be Sued

The state may sue and be sued, and the Legislature shall provide by law in what manner and in what courts suits shall be brought.

Section 23. Jurisdiction of Judges at Chambers

The several judges of the courts of record shall have such jurisdiction at chambers as may be provided by law.

Section 24. Style of Process

All process shall run in the name of "The State of Nebraska," and all prosecutions shall be carried on in the name of "The State of Nebraska."

Section 25. Supreme Court to Promulgate Rules of Practice; to Make Recommendations to Legislature

For the effectual administration of justice and the prompt disposition of judicial proceedings, the supreme court may promulgate rules of practice and procedure for all courts, uniform as to each class of courts, and not in conflict with laws governing such matters. To the same end, the court may, and when requested by the Legislature by resolution shall, certify to the Legislature its conclusions as to desirable amendments or changes in the general laws governing such practice and proceedings.

Section 26. Supreme Court to Promulgate Rules of Practice; to Make Recommendations to Legislature

Proviso as to effect of amendment. If the foregoing amendment shall be adopted by the electors, all existing courts which are not in the foregoing amendment specifically enumerated and concerning which no other provision is herein made, shall continue in existence and exercise their present jurisdiction, and the judges thereof shall receive their present compensation, until otherwise provided by law; and such judges or appointees to fill vacancies shall hold their offices until their successors shall be elected and qualified.

Section 27. Juvenile Courts; Authorization

Notwithstanding the provisions of section 9 of this Article, the Legislature may establish courts to be known as juvenile courts, with such jurisdiction and powers as the Legislature may provide. The term, qualification, compensation, and method of appointment or election of the judges of such courts, and the rules governing proceedings therein, may be fixed by the Legislature. The state shall be divided into juvenile court judicial districts that correspond to district court judicial districts until otherwise provided by law. No such court shall be established or afterwards abolished in any juvenile court judicial district unless approved by a majority of those voting on the issue.

Section 28. Commission on Judicial Qualifications; Appointment; Composition; Qualifications

The Legislature shall provide for a Commission on Judicial Qualifications consisting of:

(1) Three judges, including one district court judge, one county court judge, and one judge of any other court inferior to the Supreme Court as now exists or may hereafter be created by law, all of whom shall be appointed by the Chief Justice of the Supreme Court;

(2) three members of the Nebraska State Bar Association who shall have practiced law in this state for at least ten years and who shall be appointed by the Executive Council of the Nebraska State Bar Association;

(3) three citizens, none of whom shall be a Justice or Judge of the Supreme Court or judge of any court, active or retired, nor a member of the Nebraska State Bar Association, and who shall be appointed by the Governor; and

(4) the Chief Justice of the Supreme Court, who shall serve as its chairperson.

Section 29. Commission on Judicial Qualifications; Vote of majority Required for Action

The commission shall act by a vote of the majority of its members and no action of the commission shall be valid unless concurred in by the majority of its members.

Section 30. Judges; Discipline; Removal from Office; Grounds; Procedure

(1) A Justice or Judge of the Supreme Court or judge of any court of this state may be reprimanded, disciplined, censured, suspended without pay for a definite period of time, not to exceed six months, or removed from office for :

(a) willful misconduct in office,

(b) willful disregard of or failure to perform his or her duties,

(c) habitual intemperance,

(d) conviction of a crime involving moral turpitude,

(e) disbarment as a member of the legal profession licensed to practice law in the State of Nebraska, or

(f) conduct prejudicial to the administration of justice that brings the judicial office into disrepute, or he or she may be retired for physical or mental disability seriously interfering with the performance of his or her duties if such disability is determined to be permanent or reasonably likely to become permanent. Any citizen of the State of Nebraska may request the Commission on Judicial Qualifications to consider the qualifications of any Justice or Judge of the Supreme Court or other judge, and in such event the commission shall make such investigation as the commission deems necessary and shall, upon a finding of probable cause, reprimand such Justice or Judge of the Supreme Court or other judge or order a formal open hearing to be held before it concerning the reprimand, discipline, censure, suspension, removal, or retirement of such Justice or Judge of the Supreme Court or other judge. In the alternative or in addition, the commission may request the Supreme Court to appoint one or more special masters who shall be judges of courts of record to hold a formal open hearing to take evidence in any such matter, and to report to the commission. If, after formal open hearing, or after considering the record and report of the masters, the commission finds that the charges are established by clear and convincing evidence, it shall recommend to the Supreme Court that the Justice or Judge of the Supreme Court or other judge involved shall be reprimanded, disciplined, censured, suspended without pay for a definite period of time not to exceed six months, removed, or retired as the case may be.

(2) The Supreme Court shall review the record of the proceedings and in its discretion may permit the introduction of additional evidence. The Supreme Court shall make such determination as it finds just and proper, and may order the reprimand, discipline, censure, suspension, removal, or retirement of such Justice or Judge of the Supreme Court or other judge, or may wholly reject the recommendation. Upon an order for retirement, the Justice or Judge of the Supreme Court or other judge shall thereby be retired with the same rights and privileges as if he or she had retired pursuant to statute. Upon an order for removal, the Justice or Judge of the Supreme Court or other judge shall be removed from office, his or her salary shall cease from the date of such order, and he or she shall be ineligible for judicial office. Upon an order for suspension, the Justice or Judge of the Supreme Court or other judge shall draw no salary and shall perform no judicial functions during the period of suspension. Suspension shall not create a vacancy in the office of Justice or Judge of the Supreme Court or other judge.

(3) Upon order of the Supreme Court, a Justice or Judge of the Supreme Court or other judge shall be disqualified from acting as a Justice or Judge of the Supreme Court or other judge, without loss of salary, while there is pending (a) an indictment or information charging him or her in the United States with a crime punishable as a felony under Nebraska or federal law or (b) a recommendation to the Supreme Court by the Commission on Judicial Qualifications for his or her removal or retirement.

(4) In addition to the procedure set forth in subsections (1) and (2) of this section, on recommendation of the Commission on Judicial Qualifications or on its own motion, the Supreme Court

(a) shall remove a Justice or Judge of the Supreme Court or other judge from office when in any court in the United States such justice or judge pleads guilty or no contest to a crime punishable as a felony under Nebraska or federal law, and

(b) may suspend a Justice or Judge of the Supreme Court or other judge from office without salary when in any court in the United States such justice or judge is found guilty of a crime punishable as a felony under Nebraska or federal law or of any other crime that involves moral turpitude. If his or her conviction is reversed, suspension shall terminate and he or she shall be paid his or her salary for the period of suspension. If he or she is suspended and his or her conviction becomes final the Supreme Court shall remove him or her from office.

(5) All papers filed with and proceedings before the commission or masters appointed by the Supreme Court pursuant to this section prior to a reprimand or formal open hearing shall be confidential. The filing of papers with and the testimony given before the commission or masters or the Supreme Court shall be deemed a privileged communication.

When the Commission on Judicial Qualifications determines that disciplinary action is warranted, whether it be a reprimand or otherwise, the Commission on Judicial Qualifications shall issue one or more short announcements confirming that a complaint has been filed; stating the subject and nature of the complaint, the disciplinary action recommended or reprimand issued, or the date of the hearing; clarifying the procedural aspects; and reciting the right of a judge to a fair hearing.

When the Commission on Judicial Qualifications determines that disciplinary action is not warranted, and the existence of any investigation or complaint has become publicly known, the judge against whom a complaint has been filed or investigation commenced may waive the confidentiality of papers and proceedings under this subsection.

The Supreme Court shall by rule provide for procedure under this section before the commission, the masters, and the Supreme Court.

(6) No Justice or Judge of the Supreme Court or other judge shall participate, as a member of the commission, or as a master, or as a member of the Supreme Court, in any proceedings involving his or her own reprimand, discipline, censure, suspension, removal, or retirement.

Section 31. Judges; Procedure for Removal from Office Cumulative

These amendments are alternative to and cumulative with the methods of removal of Justices and judges provided in Article III, section 17, and Article IV, section 5, of this Constitution, and any other provision of law relating to the methods and manner of the removal of Justices, Judges, and judges of the courts of this state.

Article VI: Suffrage

Section 1. Qualifications of Electors

Every citizen of the United States who has attained the age of eighteen years on or before the first Tuesday after the first Monday in November and has resided within the state and the county and voting precinct for the terms provided by law shall, except as provided in section 2 of this article, be an elector for the calendar year in which such citizen has attained the age of eighteen years and for all succeeding calendar years.

Section 2. Who Disqualified

No person shall be qualified to vote who is non compos mentis, or who has been convicted of treason or felony under the laws of the state or of the United States, unless restored to civil rights.

Section 3. Military or Naval Service; Place and Manner of Voting

Every elector in the military or naval service of the United States or of this state may exercise the right of suffrage at such place and under such regulations as may be provided by law.

Section 4. Repealed.

Section 5. Electors; Privileged from Arrest.

Electors shall in all cases, except treason, felony, or breach of the peace, be privileged from arrest during their attendance at elections, and going to and returning from the same.

Section 6. Votes, How Cast

All votes shall be by ballot or by other means authorized by the Legislature whereby the vote and the secrecy of the elector's vote will be preserved.

Article VII: Education

Section 1. Legislature; Free Instruction in Common Schools; Provide

The Legislature shall provide for the free instruction in the common schools of this state of all persons between the ages of five and twenty-one years. The Legislature may provide for the education of other persons in educational institutions owned and controlled by the state or a political subdivision thereof.

Section 2. State Department of Education; General Supervision of School System

The State Department of Education shall be comprised of a State Board of Education and a Commissioner of Education. The State Department of Education shall have general supervision and administration of the school system of the state and of such other activities as the Legislature may direct.

Section 3. State Board of Education; Members; Election; Manner of Election; Term of Office

The State Board of Education shall be composed of eight members, who shall be elected from eight districts of substantially equal population as provided by the Legislature. Their term of office shall be for four years each. Their duties and powers shall be prescribed by the Legislature, and they shall receive no compensation, but shall be reimbursed their actual expense incurred in the performance of their duties. The members of the State Board of Education shall not be actively engaged in the educational profession and they shall be elected on a nonpartisan ballot.

Section 4. State Board of Education; Commissioner of Education; Appointment; Powers; Duties

The State Board of Education shall appoint and fix the compensation of the Commissioner of Education, who shall be the executive officer of the State Board of Education and the administrative head of the State Department of Education, and who shall have such powers and duties as the Legislature may direct. The board shall appoint all employees of the State Department of Education on the recommendation of the Commissioner of Education.

Section 5. Fines, Penalties, and License Money; Allocation; Use of Forfeited Conveyances

(1) Except as provided in subsections (2) and (3) of this section, all fines, penalties, and license money arising under the general laws of the state, except fines and penalties for violation of laws prohibiting the overloading of vehicles used upon the public roads and highways of this state, shall belong and be paid over to the counties respectively where the same may be levied or imposed, and all fines, penalties, and license money arising under the rules, bylaws, or ordinances of cities, villages, precincts, or other municipal subdivision less than a county shall belong and be paid over to the same respectively. All such fines, penalties, and license money shall be appropriated exclusively to the use and support of the common schools in the respective subdivisions where the same may accrue, except that all fines and penalties for violation of laws prohibiting the overloading of vehicles used upon the public roads and highways shall be placed as follows: Seventy-five per cent in a fund for state highways and twenty-five per cent to the county general fund where the fine or penalty is paid.

(2) Fifty per cent of all money forfeited or seized pursuant to enforcement of the drug laws shall belong and be paid over to the counties for drug enforcement purposes as the Legislature may provide.

(3) Law enforcement agencies may use conveyances forfeited pursuant to enforcement of the drug laws as the Legislature may provide. Upon the sale of such conveyances, the proceeds shall be appropriated exclusively to the use and support of the common schools as provided in subsection (1) of this section.[1]

Section 6. Educational Lands; Management; Board of Educational Lands and Funds; Members; Appointment; Sale of Lands

No lands now owned or hereafter acquired by the state for educational purposes shall be sold except at public auction under such conditions as the Legislature shall provide. The general management of all lands set apart for educational purposes shall be vested, under the direction of the Legislature, in a board of five members to be known as the Board of Educational Lands and Funds. The members shall be appointed by the Governor, subject to the approval of the Legislature, with such qualifications and for such terms and compensation as the Legislature may provide.

Section 7. Perpetual Funds Enumerated

The following are hereby declared to be perpetual funds for common school purposes, including early childhood educational purposes operated by or distributed through the common schools, of which the annual interest or income only can be appropriated, to wit:

First. Such percent as has been, or may hereafter be, granted by Congress on the sale of lands in this state.

Second. All money arising from the sale or leasing of sections number sixteen and thirty-six in each township in this state, and the lands selected, or that may be selected, in lieu thereof.

Third. The proceeds of all lands that have been, or may hereafter be, granted to this state, where by the terms and conditions of such grant the same are not to be otherwise appropriated.

Fourth. The net proceeds of lands and other property and effects that may come to this state, by escheat or forfeiture, or from unclaimed dividends, or distributive shares of the estates of deceased persons.

Fifth. All other property of any kind now belonging to the perpetual fund.

Section 8. Trust Funds Belong to State for Educational Purposes; Use; Investment

All funds belonging to the state for common school purposes, including early childhood educational purposes operated by or distributed through the common schools, the interest and income whereof only are to be used, shall be deemed trust funds. Such funds with the interest and income thereof are hereby solemnly pledged to the purposes for which they are granted and set apart and shall not be transferred to any other fund for other uses. The state shall supply any net aggregate losses thereof realized at the close of each calendar year that may in any manner accrue. Notwithstanding any other provisions in this Constitution, such funds shall be invested as the Legislature may by statute provide.

Section 9. Educational Funds; Trust Funds; Use; Early Childhood Education Endowment Fund; Created; Use; Early Childhood Education, Defined

(1) The following funds shall be exclusively used for the support and maintenance of the common schools in each school district in the state or for early childhood education operated by or distributed through the common schools as provided in subsection (3) of this section, as the Legislature shall provide:

(a) Income arising from the perpetual funds;

(b) The income from the unsold school lands, except that costs of administration shall be deducted from the income before it is so applied;

(c) All other grants, gifts, and devises that have been or may hereafter be made to the state which are not otherwise appropriated by the terms of the grant, gift, or devise; and

(d) Such other support as the Legislature may provide.

(2) No distribution or appropriation shall be made to any school district for the year in which school is not maintained for the minimum term required by law.

(3)(a) An early childhood education endowment fund shall be created for the purpose of supporting early childhood education in this state as provided by the Legislature.

(b) An amount equal to forty million dollars of the funds belonging to the state for common school and early childhood educational purposes operated by or distributed through the common schools described in Article VII, section 7, of this Constitution shall be allocated for the early childhood education endowment fund.

(c) Only interest or income on such early childhood education endowment fund may be appropriated as provided by the Legislature for the benefit of the common schools and for the exclusive purpose of supporting early childhood education in this state.

(d) For purposes of Article VII of this Constitution, early childhood education means programs operated by or distributed through the common schools promoting development and learning for children from birth to kindergarten-entrance age.

(e) If the annual income from twenty million dollars of private funding is not irrevocably committed by July 1, 2011, to the use of the early childhood education endowment fund, then the forty-million-dollar allocation pursuant to subdivision (3)(b) of this section may revert to the use of the common schools as the Legislature shall determine.

Section 10. University of Nebraska; Government; Board of Regents; Election; Student Membership; Terms

The general government of the University of Nebraska shall, under the direction of the Legislature, be vested in a board of not less than six nor more than eight regents to be designated the Board of Regents of the University of Nebraska, who shall be elected from and by districts as herein provided and three students of the University of Nebraska who shall serve as nonvoting members. Such nonvoting student members shall consist of the student body president of the University of Nebraska at Lincoln, the student body president of the University of Nebraska at Omaha, and the student body president of the University of Nebraska Medical Center. The terms of office of elected members shall be for six years each. The terms of office of student members shall be for the period of service as student body president. Their duties and powers shall be prescribed by law; and they shall receive no compensation, but may be reimbursed their actual expenses incurred in the discharge of their duties.

The Legislature shall divide the state, along county lines, into as many compact regent districts, as there are regents provided by the Legislature, of approximately equal population, which shall be numbered consecutively.

The Legislature shall redistrict the state after each federal decennial census. Such districts shall not be changed except upon the concurrence of a majority of the members of the Legislature. In any such redistricting, county lines shall be followed whenever practicable, but other established lines may be followed at the discretion of the Legislature. Whenever the state is so redistricted the members elected prior to the redistricting shall continue in office, and the law providing for such redistricting shall where necessary specify the newly established district which they shall represent for the balance of their term.

Section 11. Appropriation of Public Funds; Handicapped Children; Sectarian Instruction; Religious Test of Teacher or Student

Notwithstanding any other provision in the Constitution, appropriation of public funds shall not be made to any school or institution of learning not owned or exclusively controlled by the state or a political subdivision thereof; Provided, that the Legislature may provide that the state or any political subdivision thereof may contract with institutions not wholly owned or controlled by the state or any political subdivision to provide for educational or other services for the benefit of children under the age of twenty-one years who are handicapped, as that term is from time to time defined by the Legislature, if such services are nonsectarian in nature.

All public schools shall be free of sectarian instruction.
The state shall not accept money or property to be used for sectarian purposes; Provided, that the Legislature may provide that the state may receive money from the federal government and distribute it in accordance with the terms of any such federal grants, but no public funds of the state, any political subdivision, or any public corporation may be added thereto.
A religious test or qualification shall not be required of any teacher or student for admission or continuance in any school or institution supported in whole or in part by public funds or taxation.

Section 12. Education and Reform of Minors

The Legislature may provide by law for the establishment of a school or schools for the safe keeping, education, employment and reformation of all children under the age of eighteen years, who, for want of proper parental care, or other cause, are growing up in mendicancy or crime.

Section 13. State Colleges; Government; Board; Name; Selection; Duties; Compensation

The general government of the state colleges as now existing, and such other state colleges as may be established by law, shall be vested, under the direction of the Legislature, in a board of seven members to be styled as designated by the Legislature, six of whom shall be appointed by the Governor, with the advice and consent of the Legislature, two each for a term of two, four, and six years, and two each biennium thereafter for a term of six years, and the Commissioner of Education shall be a member ex officio. The duties and powers of the board shall be prescribed by law, and the members thereof shall receive no compensation for the performance of their duties, but may be reimbursed their actual expenses incurred therein.

Section 14. Coordinating Commission for Postsecondary Education; Membership; Powers and Duties; Coordination, Defined

On January 1, 1992, there shall be established the Coordinating Commission for Postsecondary Education which shall, under the direction of the Legislature, be vested with the authority for the coordination of public postsecondary educational institutions. Public postsecondary educational institutions shall include each postsecondary educational campus or institution which is governed by the Board of Regents of the University of Nebraska, the Board of Trustees of the Nebraska State Colleges, any board or boards established for the community colleges, or any other governing board for any other public postsecondary educational institution which may be established by the Legislature. Coordination shall mean:

(1) Authority to adopt, and revise as needed, a comprehensive statewide plan for postsecondary education which shall include

(a) definitions of the role and mission of each public postsecondary educational institution within any general assignments of role and mission as may be prescribed by the Legislature and

(b) plans for facilities which utilize tax funds designated by the Legislature;

(2) Authority to review, monitor, and approve or disapprove each public postsecondary educational institution's programs and capital construction projects which utilize tax funds designated by the Legislature in order to provide compliance and consistency with the comprehensive plan and to prevent unnecessary duplication; and

(3) Authority to review and modify, if needed to promote compliance and consistency with the comprehensive statewide plan and prevent unnecessary duplication, the budget requests of the Board of Regents of the University of Nebraska, the Board of Trustees of the Nebraska State Colleges, any board or boards established for the community colleges, or any other governing board for any other public postsecondary educational institution which may be established by the Legislature.

The Legislature may provide the commission with additional powers and duties related to postsecondary education as long as such powers and duties do not invade the governance and management authority of the Board of Regents of the University of Nebraska and the Board of Trustees of the Nebraska State Colleges as provided in the Constitution of Nebraska, Article VII, sections 10 and 13. The Legislature may provide that coordination of the community colleges by the commission pursuant to this section may be conducted through a board or

association representing all the community colleges.
Nothing in this section providing for statewide coordination shall limit or require the use of property tax revenue by and for community colleges.

The commission shall consist of eleven members, residents of the state or the districts for which appointed, who shall be appointed by the Governor with the approval of a majority of the Legislature. Six of the members shall be chosen from six districts of approximately equal population and five shall be chosen on a statewide basis.

The terms of the members of the commission shall be six years or until a successor is qualified and takes office, except that of the members initially appointed, four members shall serve for terms of two years and four members shall serve for terms of four years. The members of the commission shall receive no compensation for the performance of their duties but may be reimbursed their actual and necessary expenses.

Section 15. Omitted.

Section 16. Repealed

Section 17. Repealed.

Article VIII: Revenue

Section 1. Revenue; Raised by Taxation; Legislative Powers

The necessary revenue of the state and its governmental subdivisions shall be raised by taxation in such manner as the Legislature may direct. Notwithstanding Article I, section 16, Article III, section 18, or Article VIII, section 4, of this Constitution or any other provision of this Constitution to the contrary:

(1) Taxes shall be levied by valuation uniformly and proportionately upon all real property and franchises as defined by the Legislature except as otherwise provided in or permitted by this Constitution;

(2) tangible personal property, as defined by the Legislature, not exempted by this Constitution or by legislation, shall all be taxed at depreciated cost using the same depreciation method with reasonable class lives, as determined by the Legislature, or shall all be taxed by valuation uniformly and proportionately;

(3) the Legislature may provide for a different method of taxing motor vehicles and may also establish a separate class of motor vehicles consisting of those owned and held for resale by motor vehicle dealers which shall be taxed in the manner and to the extent provided by the Legislature and may also establish a separate class for trucks, trailers, semitrailers, truck-tractors, or combinations thereof, consisting of those owned by residents and nonresidents of this state, and operating in interstate commerce, and may provide reciprocal and proportionate taxation of such vehicles. The tax proceeds from motor vehicles taxed in each county shall be allocated to the county and the cities, villages, and school districts of such county;

(4) the Legislature may provide that agricultural land and horticultural land, as defined by the Legislature, shall constitute a separate and distinct class of property for purposes of taxation and may provide for a different method of taxing agricultural land and horticultural land which results in values that are not uniform and proportionate with all other real property and franchises but which results in values that are uniform and proportionate upon all property within the class of agricultural land and horticultural land;

(5) the Legislature may enact laws to provide that the value of land actively devoted to agricultural or horticultural use shall for property tax purposes be that value which such land has for agricultural or horticultural use without regard to any value which such land might have for other purposes or uses;

(6) the Legislature may prescribe standards and methods for the determination of the value of real property at uniform and proportionate values;

(7) in furtherance of the purposes for which such a law of the United States has been adopted, whenever there exists a law of the United States which is intended to protect a specifically designated type, use, user, or owner of property or franchise from discriminatory state or local taxation, such property or franchise shall constitute a separate class of property or franchise under the laws of the State of Nebraska, and such property or franchise may not be taken into consideration in determining whether taxes are levied by valuation uniformly or proportionately upon any property or franchise, and the Legislature may enact laws which statutorily recognize such class and which tax or exempt from taxation such class of property or franchise in such manner as it determines; and

(8) the Legislature may provide that livestock shall constitute a separate and distinct class of property for purposes of taxation and may further provide for reciprocal and proportionate taxation of livestock located in this state for only part of a year. Each actual property tax rate levied for a governmental subdivision shall be the same for all classes of taxed property and franchises. Taxes uniform as to class of property or the ownership or use thereof may be levied by valuation or otherwise upon classes of intangible property as the Legislature may determine, and such intangible property held in trust or otherwise for the purpose of funding pension, profit-sharing, or other employee benefit plans as defined by the Legislature may be declared exempt from taxation. Taxes other than property taxes may be authorized by law. Existing revenue laws shall continue in effect until changed by the Legislature.

Section 2. Exemption of Property from Taxation; Classification

Notwithstanding Article I, section 16, Article III, section 18, or Article VIII, section 1 or 4, of this Constitution or any other provision of this Constitution to the contrary:

(1) The property of the state and its governmental subdivisions shall constitute a separate class of property and shall be exempt from taxation to the extent such property is used by the state or governmental subdivision for public purposes authorized to the state or governmental subdivision by this Constitution or the Legislature. To the extent such property is not used for the authorized public purposes, the Legislature may classify such property, exempt such classes, and impose or authorize some or all of such property to be subject to property taxes or payments in lieu of property taxes except as provided by law;

(2) the Legislature by general law may classify and exempt from taxation property owned by and used exclusively for agricultural and horticultural societies and property owned and used exclusively for educational, religious, charitable, or cemetery purposes, when such property is not owned or used for financial gain or profit to either the owner or user;

(3) household goods and personal effects, as defined by law, may be exempted from taxation in whole or in part, as may be provided by general law, and the Legislature may prescribe a formula for the determination of value of household goods and personal effects;

(4) the Legislature by general law may provide that the increased value of land by reason of shade or ornamental trees planted along the highway shall not be taken into account in the assessment of such land;

(5) the Legislature, by general law and upon any terms, conditions, and restrictions it prescribes, may provide that the increased value of real property resulting from improvements designed primarily for energy conservation may be exempt from taxation;

(6) the value of a home substantially contributed by the United States Department of Veterans Affairs for a paraplegic veteran or multiple amputee shall be exempt from taxation during the life of such veteran or until the death or remarriage of his or her surviving spouse;

(7) the Legislature may exempt from an intangible property tax life insurance and life insurance annuity contracts and any payment connected therewith and any right to pension or retirement payments;

(8) the Legislature may exempt inventory from taxation;

(9) the Legislature may define and classify personal property in such manner as it sees fit, whether by type, use, user, or owner, and may exempt any such class or classes of property from taxation if such exemption is reasonable or may exempt all personal property from taxation;

(10) no property shall be exempt from taxation except as permitted by or as provided in this Constitution;

(11) the Legislature may by general law provide that a portion of the value of any residence actually occupied as a homestead by any classification of owners as determined by the Legislature shall be exempt from taxation; and

(12) the Legislature may by general law, and upon any terms, conditions, and restrictions it prescribes, provide that the increased value of real property resulting from improvements designed primarily for the purpose of renovating, rehabilitating, or preserving historically significant real property may be, in whole or in part, exempt from taxation.

Section 3. Redemption from Sales of Real Estate for Taxes

The right of redemption from all sales of real estate, for the non-payment of taxes or special assessments of any character whatever, shall exist in favor of owners and persons interested in such real estate, for a period of not less than two years from such sales thereof. Provided, that occupants shall in all cases be served with personal notice before the time of redemption expires.

Section 4. Legislature Has No Power to Remit Taxes; Exception; Cancellation of Taxes on Land Acquired by the State

Except as to tax and assessment charges against real property remaining delinquent and unpaid for a period of fifteen years or longer, the Legislature shall have no power to release or discharge any county, city, township, town, or district whatever, or the inhabitants thereof, or any corporation, or the property therein, from their or its proportionate share of taxes to be levied for state purposes, or due any municipal corporation, nor shall commutation for such taxes be authorized in any form whatever;

Provided, that the Legislature may provide by law for the payment or cancellation of taxes or assessments against real estate remaining unpaid against real estate owned or acquired by the state or its governmental subdivisions.

Section 5. County Taxes; Limitation

County authorities shall never assess taxes the aggregate of which shall exceed fifty cents per one hundred dollars of taxable value as determined by the assessment rolls, except for the payment of indebtedness existing at the adoption hereof, unless authorized by a vote of the people of the county.

Section 6. Local Improvements of Cities, Towns and Villages

The Legislature may vest the corporate authorities of cities, towns and villages, with power to make local improvements, including facilities for providing off-street parking for vehicles, by special assessments or by special taxation of property benefited, and to redetermine and reallocate from time to time the benefits arising from the acquisition of such off-street parking facilities, and the Legislature may vest the corporate authorities of cities and villages with power to levy special assessments for the maintenance, repair and reconstruction of such off-street parking facilities. For all other corporate purposes, all municipal corporations may be vested with authority to assess and collect taxes, but such taxes shall be uniform in respect to persons and property within the jurisdiction of the body imposing the same, except that cities and villages may be empowered by the Legislature to assess and collect separate and additional taxes within off-street parking districts created by and within any city or village on such terms as the Legislature may prescribe.

Section 7. Private Property Not Liable for Corporate Debts; Municipalities and Inhabitants Exempt for Corporate Purposes

Private property shall not be liable to be taken or sold for the payment of the corporate debts of municipal corporations. The Legislature shall not impose taxes upon municipal corporations, or the inhabitants or property thereof, for corporate purposes.

Section 8. Funding Indebtedness; Warrants

The Legislature at its first session shall provide by law for the funding of all outstanding warrants, and other indebtedness of the state, at a rate of interest not exceeding eight per cent per annum.

Section 9. Claims upon Treasury; Adjustment; Approval; Appeal

The Legislature shall provide by law that all claims upon the treasury shall be examined and adjusted as the Legislature may provide before any warrant for the amount allowed shall be drawn. Any party aggrieved by the action taken on a claim in which he has an interest may appeal to the district court.

Section 10. Taxation of Grain and Seed; Alternative Basis Permitted

Notwithstanding the other provisions of Article VIII, the Legislature is authorized to substitute a basis other than valuation for taxes upon grain and seed produced or handled in this state. Existing revenue laws not inconsistent with the Constitution shall continue in effect until changed by the Legislature.

Section 11. Public Corporations and Political Subdivisions Providing Electricity; Payment in Lieu of Taxes

Every public corporation and political subdivision organized primarily to provide electricity or irrigation and electricity shall annually make the same payments in lieu of taxes as it made in 1957, which payments shall be allocated in the same proportion to the same public bodies or their successors as they were in 1957.

The legislature may require each such public corporation to pay to the treasurer of any county in which may be located any incorporated city or village, within the limits of which such public corporation sells electricity at retail, a sum equivalent to five (5) per cent of the annual gross revenue of such public corporation derived from retail sales of electricity within such city or village, less an amount equivalent to the 1957 payments in lieu of taxes made by such public corporation with respect to property or operations in any such city or village. The payments in lieu of tax as made in 1957, together with any payments made as authorized in this section shall be in lieu of all other taxes, payments in lieu of taxes, franchise payments, occupation and excise taxes, but shall not be in lieu of motor vehicle licenses and wheel taxes, permit fees, gasoline tax and other such excise taxes or general sales taxes levied against the public generally. So much of such five (5) per cent as is in excess of an amount equivalent to the amount paid by such public corporation in lieu of taxes in 1957 shall be distributed in each year to the city or village, the school districts located in such city or village, the county in which such city or village is located, and the State of Nebraska, in the proportion that their respective property tax mill levies in each such year bear to the total of such mill levies.

Section 12. Cities or Villages; Redevelopment Project; Substandard and Blighted Property; Incur Indebtedness; Taxes; How Treated

For the purpose of rehabilitating, acquiring, or redeveloping substandard and blighted property in a redevelopment project as determined by law, any city or village of the state may, notwithstanding any other provision in the Constitution, and without regard to charter limitations and restrictions, incur indebtedness, whether by bond, loans, notes, advance of money, or otherwise. Notwithstanding any other provision in the Constitution or a local charter, such cities or villages may also pledge for and apply to the payment of the principal, interest, and any premium on such indebtedness all taxes levied by all taxing bodies, which taxes shall be at such rate for a period not to exceed fifteen years, on the assessed valuation of the property in the project area portion of a designated blighted and substandard area that is in excess of the assessed valuation of such property for the year prior to such rehabilitation, acquisition, or redevelopment.

When such indebtedness and the interest thereon have been paid in full, such property thereafter shall be taxed as is other property in the respective taxing jurisdictions and such taxes applied as all other taxes of the respective taxing bodies.

Section 13. Revenue Laws and Legislative Acts; How Construed

Notwithstanding Article I, section 16, Article III, section 18, or Article VIII, section 1 or 4, of this Constitution or any other provision of this Constitution to the contrary, amendments to Article VIII of this Constitution passed in 1992 shall be effective from and after January 1, 1992, and existing revenue laws and legislative acts passed in the regular legislative session of 1992, not inconsistent with this Constitution as amended, shall be considered ratified and confirmed by such amendments without the need for legislative reenactment of such laws.

Article IX: Counties

Section 1. Area

No new county shall be formed or established by the legislature which will reduce the county or counties, or either of them to a less area than four hundred square miles, nor shall any county be formed of a less area.

Section 2. Division of County; Decision of Question

No county shall be divided nor any part of the territory of any county be stricken therefrom, nor shall any county or part of the territory of any county be added to an adjoining county without submitting the question to the qualified electors of each county affected thereby, nor unless approved by a majority of the qualified electors of each county voting thereon; provided, that when county boundaries divide sections, or overlap, or fail to meet, or are in doubt, the Legislature may by law provide for their adjustment, but in all cases the new boundary shall follow the nearest section line or the thread of the main channel of a boundary stream.

Section 3. County Added to Another; Prior Indebtedness; County Stricken Off; Liabilities

When a county shall be added to another, all prior indebtedness of each county shall remain a charge on the taxable property within the territory of each county as it existed prior to consolidation. When any part of a county is stricken off and attached to another county, the part stricken off shall be holden for its proportion of all then existing liabilities of the county from which it is taken, but shall not be holden for any then existing liabilities of the county to which it is attached.

Section 4. County and Township Officers

The Legislature shall provide by law for the election of such county and township officers as may be necessary and for the consolidation of county offices for two or more counties; Provided, that each of the counties affected may disapprove such consolidation by a majority vote in each of such counties.

Section 5. Township Organization

The Legislature shall provide by general law for township organization, under which any county may organize whenever a majority of the legal voters of such county voting at any general election shall so determine; and in any county that shall have adopted a township organization the question of continuing the same may be submitted to a vote of the electors of such county at a general election in the manner that shall be provided by law.

Article X: Public Service Corporations

Section 1. Reports Under Oath

Every public utility corporation or common carrier organized or doing business in this state shall report, under oath, to the Railway Commission, when required by law or the order of said Commission. The reports so made shall include such matter as may be required by law or the order of said Commission.

Section 2. Property Liable to Sale on Execution

The rolling stock and all other movable property belonging to any railroad company or corporation in this state, shall be liable to execution and sale in the same manner as the personal property of individuals, and the legislature shall pass no law exempting any such property from execution and sale.

Section 3. Consolidation of Stock or Property

No public utility corporation or common carrier shall consolidate its stock, property, franchise, or earnings in whole or in part with any other public utility corporation or common carrier owning a parallel or competing property without permission of the Railway Commission; and in no case shall any consolidation take place except upon public notice of at least sixty days to all stockholders, in such manner as may be provided by law. The Legislature may by law require all public utilities and common carriers to exchange business through physical connection, joint use, connected service, or otherwise.

Section 4. Railways Declared Public Highways; Maximum Rates; Liability Not Limited

Railways heretofore constructed, or that may hereafter be constructed, in this state are hereby declared public highways, and shall be free to all persons for the transportation of their persons and property thereon, under such regulations as may be prescribed by law. And the legislature may from time to time pass laws establishing reasonable maximum rates of charges for the transportation of passengers and freight on the different railroads in this state. The liability of railroad corporations as common carriers shall never be limited.

Section 5. Capital Stock; Dividends

The capital stock of public utility corporations or common carriers shall not be increased for any purpose, except after public notice for sixty days, and in such manner as may be provided by law. No dividend shall be declared or distributed except out of net earnings after paying all operating expenses including a depreciation reserve sufficient to keep the investment intact.

Section 6. Eminent Domain

The exercise of the power and the right of eminent domain shall never be so construed or abridged as to prevent the taking by the legislature, of the property and franchises of incorporated companies already organized, or hereafter to be organized, and subjecting them to the public necessity the same as of individuals.

Section 7. Unjust Discrimination and Extortion

The Legislature shall pass laws to correct abuses and prevent unjust discrimination and extortion in all charges of express, telegraph and railroad companies in this state and enforce such laws by adequate penalties to the extent, if necessary for that purpose, of forfeiture of their property and franchises.

Section 8. Eminent Domain for Depot or Other Uses

No railroad corporation organized under the laws of any other state, or of the United States and doing business in this state shall be entitled to exercise the right of eminent domain or have power to acquire the right of way, or real estate for depot or other uses, until it shall have become a body corporate pursuant to and in accordance with the laws of this state.

Article XI: Municipal Corporations

Section 1. Subscription to Stock Prohibited; Exception

No city, county, town, precinct, municipality, or other subdivision of the state shall ever become a subscriber to the capital stock, or owner of such stock, or any portion or interest therein of any railroad, or private corporation, or association, except that, notwithstanding any other provision of this Constitution, the Legislature may authorize the investment of public endowment funds by any city which is authorized by this Constitution to establish a charter, in the manner required of a prudent investor who shall act with care, skill, and diligence under the prevailing circumstance and in such investments as the governing body of such city, acting in a fiduciary capacity for the exclusive purpose of protecting and benefiting such investment, may determine, subject to such limitations as the Legislature may by statute provide.

Section 2. City of 5,000 May Frame Charter; Procedure

Any city having a population of more than five thousand (5000) inhabitants may frame a charter for its own government, consistent with and subject to the constitution and laws of this state, by causing a convention of fifteen freeholders, who shall have been for at least five years qualified electors thereof, to be elected by the qualified voters of said city at any general or special election, whose duty it shall be within four months after such election, to prepare and propose a charter for such city, which charter, when completed, with a prefatory synopsis, shall be signed by the officers and members of the convention, or a majority thereof, and delivered to the clerk of said city, who shall publish the same in full, with his official certification, in the official paper of said city, if there be one, and if there be no official paper, then in at least one newspaper published and in general circulation in said city, three times, and a week apart, and within not less than thirty days after such publication it shall be submitted to the qualified electors of said city at a general or special election, and if a majority of such qualified voters, voting thereon, shall ratify the same, it shall at the end of sixty days thereafter, become the charter of said city, and supersede any existing charter and all amendments thereof. A duplicate certificate shall be made, setting forth the charter proposed and its ratification (together with the vote for and against) and duly certified by the City Clerk, and authenticated by the corporate seal of said city and one copy thereof shall be filed with the Secretary of State and the other deposited among the archives of the city, and shall thereupon become and be the charter of said city, and all amendments of such charter, shall be authenticated in the same manner, and filed with the secretary of state and deposited in the archives of the city.

Section 3. Rejection of Charter; Effect; Procedure to Frame New Charter

But if said charter be rejected, then within six months thereafter, the mayor and council or governing authorities of said city may call a special election at which fifteen members of a new charter convention shall be elected to be called and held as above in such city, and they shall proceed as above to frame a charter which shall in like manner and to the like end be published and submitted to a vote of said voters for their approval or rejection. If again rejected, the procedure herein designated may be repeated until a charter is finally approved by a majority of those voting thereon, and certified (together with the vote for and against) to the secretary of state as aforesaid, and a copy thereof deposited in the archives of the city, whereupon it shall become the charter of said city. Members of each of said charter conventions shall be elected at large, and they shall complete their labors within sixty days after their respective election. The charter shall make proper provision for continuing, amending or repealing the ordinances of the city.

Section 4.Charter; Amendment; Charter Convention

Such charter so ratified and adopted may be amended, or a charter convention called, by a proposal therefore made by the law-making body of such city or by the qualified electors in number not less than five per cent of the next preceding gubernatorial vote in such city, by petition filed with the council or governing authorities. The council or governing authorities shall submit the same to a vote of the qualified electors at the next general or special election not held within thirty days after such petition is filed. In submitting any such charter or charter amendments, any alternative article or section may be presented for the choice of the voters and may be voted on separately without prejudice to others. Whenever the question of a charter convention is carried by a majority of those voting thereon, a charter convention shall be called through a special election ordinance, and the same shall be constituted and held and the proposed charter submitted to a vote of the qualified electors, approved or rejected, as provided in Section two hereof. The City Clerk of said city shall publish with his official certification, for three times, a week apart in the official paper in said city, if there be one, and if there be no official paper, then in at least one newspaper, published and in general circulation in said city, the full text of any charter or charter amendment to be voted on at any general or special election.

No charter or charter amendment adopted under the provisions of this amendment shall be amended or repealed except by electoral vote. And no such charter or charter amendment shall diminish the tax rate for state purposes fixed by act of the Legislature, or interfere in any wise with the collection of state taxes.

Section 5. Charter of City of 100,000; Home Rule Charter Authorized

The charter of any city having a population of more than one hundred thousand inhabitants may be adopted as the home rule charter of such city by a majority vote of the qualified electors of such city voting upon the question, and when so adopted may thereafter be changed or amended as provided in Section 4 of this article, subject to the Constitution and laws of the state.

Article XII: Miscellaneous Corporations

Section 1. Legislature to Provide for Organization, Regulation, and Supervision of Corporations and Associations; Limitation; Elections for Directors or Managers; Voting Right of Stockholders

The Legislature shall provide by general law for the organization, regulation, supervision and general control of all corporations, and for the organization, supervision and general control of mutual and co-operative companies and associations, and by such legislation shall insure the mutuality and co-operative features and functions thereof. Foreign corporations transacting or seeking to transact business in this state shall be subject, under general law, to regulation, supervision and general control, and shall not be given greater rights or privileges than are given domestic corporations of a similar character. No corporations shall be created by special law, nor their charters be extended, changed or amended, except those corporations organized for charitable, educational, penal or reformatory purposes, which are to be and remain under the patronage and control of the state. The Legislature shall provide by law that in all elections for directors or managers of incorporated companies every stockholder owning voting stock shall have the right to vote in person or proxy for the number of such shares owned by him, for as many persons as there are directors or managers to be elected or to cumulate such shares and give one candidate as many votes as the number of directors multiplied by the number his shares shall equal, or to distribute them upon the same principal among as many candidates as he shall think fit, and such directors or managers shall not be elected in any other manner; Provided, that any mutual or cooperative company or association may, in its articles of incorporation, limit the number of shares of stock any stockholder may own, the transfer of such stock, and the right of each stockholder or member to one vote only in the meetings of such company or association. All general laws passed pursuant to this section may be altered from time to time, or repealed.

Section 2. Repealed.

Section 3. Repealed.

Section 4. Repealed.

Section 5. Repealed.

Section 6. Repealed.

Section 7. Repealed.

Section 8. Corporation Acquiring and Interest in Real Estate Used for Farming or Ranching or Engaging in Farming or Ranching; Restrictions; Secretary of State, Attorney General; Duties; Legislature; Powers

That Article XII of the Constitution of the State of Nebraska be amended by adding a new section numbered 8 and subsections as numbered, notwithstanding any other provisions of this Constitution.

Sec. 8(1) No corporation or syndicate shall acquire, or otherwise obtain an interest, whether legal, beneficial, or otherwise, in any title to real estate used for farming or ranching in this state, or engage in farming or ranching.
Corporation shall mean any corporation organized under the laws of any state of the United States or any country or any partnership of which such corporation is a partner.
Farming or ranching shall mean

(i) the cultivation of land for the production of agricultural crops, fruit, or other horticultural products, or

(ii) the ownership, keeping or feeding of animals for the production of livestock or livestock products.

Syndicate shall mean any limited partnership organized under the laws of any state of the United States or any country, other than limited partnerships in which the partners are members of a family, or a trust created for the benefit of a member of that family, related to one another within the fourth degree of kindred according to the rules of civil law, or their spouses, at least one of whom is a person residing on or actively engaged in the day to day labor and management of the farm or ranch, and none of whom are nonresident aliens. This shall not include general partnerships.

These restrictions shall not apply to:

(A) A family farm or ranch corporation. Family farm or ranch corporation shall mean a corporation engaged in farming or ranching or the ownership of agricultural land, in which the majority of the voting stock is held by members of a family, or a trust created for the benefit of a member of that family, related to one another within the fourth degree of kindred according to the rules of civil law, or their spouses, at least one of whom is a person residing on or actively engaged in the day to day labor and management of the farm or ranch and none of whose stockholders are non-resident aliens and none of whose stockholders are corporations or partnerships, unless all of the stockholders or partners of such entities are persons related within the fourth degree of kindred to the majority of stockholders in the family farm corporation.
These restrictions shall not apply to:

(B) Non-profit corporations.

These restrictions shall not apply to:

(C) Nebraska Indian tribal corporations.
These restrictions shall not apply to:

(D) Agricultural land, which, as of the effective date of this Act, is being farmed or ranched, or which is owned or leased, or in which there is a legal or beneficial interest in title directly or indirectly owned, acquired, or obtained by a corporation or syndicate, so long as such land or other interest in title shall be held in continuous ownership or under continuous lease by the same such corporation or syndicate, and including such additional ownership or leasehold as is reasonably necessary to meet the requirements of pollution control regulations. For the purposes of this exemption, land purchased on a contract signed as of the effective date of this amendment, shall be considered as owned on the effective date of this amendment.
These restrictions shall not apply to:

(E) A farm or ranch operated for research or experimental purposes, if any commercial sales from such farm or ranch are only incidental to the research or experimental objectives of the corporation or syndicate.
These restrictions shall not apply to:

(F) Agricultural land operated by a corporation for the purpose of raising poultry.
These restrictions shall not apply to:

(G) Land leased by alfalfa processors for the production of alfalfa.
These restrictions shall not apply to:

(H) Agricultural land operated for the purpose of growing seed, nursery plants, or sod.
These restrictions shall not apply to:

(I) Mineral rights on agricultural land.
These restrictions shall not apply to:

(J) Agricultural land acquired or leased by a corporation or syndicate for immediate or potential use for nonfarming or nonranching purposes. A corporation or syndicate may hold such agricultural land in such acreage as may be necessary to its nonfarm or nonranch business operation, but pending the development of such agricultural land for nonfarm or nonranch purposes, not to exceed a period of five years, such land may not be used for farming or ranching except under lease to a family farm or ranch corporation or a non-syndicate and non-corporate farm or ranch.

These restrictions shall not apply to:

(K) Agricultural lands or livestock acquired by a corporation or syndicate by process of law in the collection of debts, or by any procedures for the enforcement of a lien, encumbrance, or claim thereon, whether created by mortgage or otherwise.

Any lands so acquired shall be disposed of within a period of five years and shall not be used for farming or ranching prior to being disposed of, except under a lease to a family farm or ranch corporation or a non-syndicate and non-corporate farm or ranch. These restrictions shall not apply to:

(L) A bona fide encumbrance taken for purposes of security.

These restrictions shall not apply to:

(M) Custom spraying, fertilizing, or harvesting.

These restrictions shall not apply to:

(N) Livestock futures contracts, livestock purchased for slaughter, or livestock purchased and resold within two weeks. If a family farm corporation, which has qualified under all the requirements of a family farm or ranch corporation, ceases to meet the defined criteria, it shall have fifty years, if the ownership of the majority of the stock of such corporation continues to be held by persons related to one another within the fourth degree of kindred or their spouses, and their landholdings are not increased, to either re-qualify as a family farm corporation or dissolve and return to personal ownership. The Secretary of State shall monitor corporate and syndicate agricultural land purchases and corporate and syndicate farming and ranching operations, and notify the Attorney General of any possible violations. If the Attorney General has reason to believe that a corporation or syndicate is violating this amendment, he or she shall commence an action in district court to enjoin any pending illegal land purchase, or livestock operation, or to force divestiture of land held in violation of this amendment. The court shall order any land held in violation of this amendment to be divested within two years. If land so ordered by the court has not been divested within two years, the court shall declare the land escheated to the State of Nebraska.

If the Secretary of State or Attorney General fails to perform his or her duties as directed by this amendment, Nebraska citizens and entities shall have standing in district court to seek enforcement.

The Nebraska Legislature may enact, by general law, further restrictions prohibiting certain agricultural operations that the legislature deems contrary to the intent of this section.

Article XIII: State, County, and Municipal Indebtedness

Section 1. State May Contract Debts; Limitation; Exceptions

The state may, to meet casual deficits, or failures in the revenue, contract debts never to exceed in the aggregate one hundred thousand dollars, and no greater indebtedness shall be incurred except for the purpose of repelling invasion, suppressing insurrection, or defending the state in war, and provision shall be made for the payment of the interest annually, as it shall accrue, by a tax levied for the purpose, or from other sources of revenue, which law providing for the payment of such interest by such tax shall be irrepealable until such debt is paid; Provided, that if the Legislature determines by a three-fifths vote of the members elected thereto that

(1) the need for construction of highways in this state requires such action, it may authorize the issuance of bonds for such construction, and for the payment of the interest and the retirement of such bonds it may pledge any tolls to be received from such highways or it may irrevocably pledge for the term of the bonds all or a part of any state revenue closely related to the use of such highways, such as motor vehicle fuel taxes or motor vehicle license fees and

(2) the construction of water retention and impoundment structures for the purposes of water conservation and management will promote the general welfare of the state, it may authorize the issuance of revenue bonds for such construction, and for the payment of the interest and the retirement of such bonds it may pledge all or any part of any state revenue derived from the use of such structures; and provided further, that the Board of Regents of the University of Nebraska, the Board of Trustees of the Nebraska State Colleges, and the State Board of Education may issue revenue bonds to construct, purchase, or otherwise acquire, extend, add to, remodel, repair, furnish, and equip dormitories, residence halls, single or multiple dwelling units, or other facilities for the housing and boarding of students, single or married, and faculty or other employees, buildings and structures for athletic purposes, student unions or centers, and for the medical care and physical development and activities of students, and buildings or other facilities for parking, which bonds shall be payable solely out of revenue, fees, and other payments derived from the use of the buildings and facilities constructed or acquired, including buildings and facilities heretofore or hereafter constructed or acquired, and paid for out of the proceeds of other issues of revenue bonds, and the revenue, fees, and payments so pledged need not be appropriated by the Legislature, and any such revenue bonds heretofore issued by either of such boards are hereby authorized, ratified, and validated. Bonds for new construction shall be first approved as the Legislature shall provide.

Section 2. Industrial and Economic Development; Powers of Counties and Municipalities

Notwithstanding any other provision in the Constitution, the Legislature may authorize any county or incorporated city or village, including cities operating under home rule charters, to acquire, own, develop, and lease real and personal property suitable for use by manufacturing or industrial enterprises and to issue revenue bonds for the purpose of defraying the cost of acquiring and developing such property by construction, purchase, or otherwise. The Legislature may also authorize such county, city, or village to acquire, own, develop, and lease real and personal property suitable for use by enterprises as determined by law if such property is located in blighted areas as determined by law and to issue revenue bonds for the purpose of defraying the cost of acquiring and developing or financing such property by construction, purchase, or otherwise. Such bonds shall not become general obligation bonds of the governmental subdivision by which such bonds are issued. Any real or personal property acquired, owned, developed, or used by any such county, city, or village pursuant to this section shall be subject to taxation to the same extent as private property during the time it is leased to or held by private interests, notwithstanding the provisions of Article VIII, section 2, of the Constitution. The acquiring, owning, developing, and leasing of such property shall be deemed for a public purpose, but the governmental subdivision shall not have the right to acquire such property by condemnation. The principal of and interest on any bonds issued may be secured by a pledge of the lease and the revenue therefrom and by mortgage upon such property. No such governmental subdivision shall have the power to operate any such property as a business or in any manner except as the lessor thereof.

Notwithstanding any other provision in the Constitution, the Legislature may also authorize any incorporated city or village, including cities operating under home rule charters, to appropriate from local sources of revenue such funds as may be deemed necessary for an economic or industrial development project or program subject to approval by a vote of a majority of the registered voters of such city or village voting upon the question. For purposes of this provision, funds from local sources of revenue shall mean funds raised from general taxes levied by the city or village and shall not include any funds received by the city or village which are derived from state or federal sources.[1]

Section 3. Credit of State; Exception

The credit of the state shall never be given or loaned in aid of any individual, association, or corporation, except that the state may guarantee or make long-term, low-interest loans to Nebraska residents seeking adult or post high school education at any public or private institution in this state. Qualifications for and the repayment of such loans shall be as prescribed by the Legislature.

Article XIV: Militia

Section 1. Personnel; Organization; Discipline

The Legislature may provide for the personnel, organization, and discipline of the militia of the state.

Article XV: Miscellaneous Provisions

Section 1. Official Oath; Refusal: Disqualification

Executive and judicial officers and members of the legislature, before they enter upon their official duties shall take and subscribe the following oath, or affirmation. "I do solemnly swear (or affirm) that I will support the constitution of the United States, and the constitution of the State of Nebraska, and will faithfully discharge the duties of .... according to the best of my ability, and that at the election at which I was chosen to fill said office, I have not improperly influenced in any way the vote of any elector, and have not accepted, nor will I accept or receive, directly or indirectly, any money or other valuable thing from any corporation, company or person, or any promise of office, for any official act or influence (for any vote I may give or withhold on any bill, resolution, or appropriation)." Any such officer or member of the legislature who shall refuse to take the oath herein prescribed, shall forfeit his office, and any person who shall be convicted of having sworn falsely to, or of violating his said oath shall forfeit his office, and thereafter be disqualified from holding any office of profit or trust in this state unless he shall have been restored to civil rights.

Section 2. Official in Default as Collector and Custodian of Public Money or Property; Disqualification; Felon Disqualified

No person who is in default as collector and custodian of public money or property shall be eligible to any office of trust or profit under the constitution or laws of this state. No person convicted of a felony shall be eligible to any such office unless he shall have been restored to civil rights.

Section 3. Repealed.

Section 4. Water a Public Necessity

The necessity of water for domestic use and for irrigation purposes in the State of Nebraska is hereby declared to be a natural want.

Section 5. Use of Water Dedicated to People

The use of the water of every natural stream within the State of Nebraska is hereby dedicated to the people of the state for beneficial purposes, subject to the provisions of the following section.

Section 6. Right to Divert Unappropriated Waters

The right to divert unappropriated waters of every natural stream for beneficial use shall never be denied except when such denial is demanded by the public interest. Priority of appropriation shall give the better right as between those using the water for the same purpose, but when the waters of any natural stream are not sufficient for the use of all those desiring to use the same, those using the water for domestic purposes shall have preference over those claiming it for any other purpose, and those using the water for agricultural purposes shall have the preference over those using the same for manufacturing purposes. Provided, no inferior right to the use of the waters of this state shall be acquired by a superior right without just compensation therefore to the inferior user.

Section 7. Use of Water for Power Purposes.

The use of the waters of the state for power purposes shall be deemed a public use and shall never be alienated, but may be leased or otherwise developed as by law prescribed.

Section 8. Employment of Women and Children; Minimum Wage

Laws may be enacted regulating the hours and conditions of employment of women and children, and securing to such employees a proper minimum wage.

Section 9. Controversies Between Employers and Employees; Industrial Commission; Appeals

Laws may be enacted providing for the investigation, submission, and determination of controversies between employers and employees in any business or vocation affected with a public interest and for the prevention of unfair business practices and unconscionable gains in any business or vocation affecting the public welfare. An Industrial Commission may be created for the purpose of administering such laws, and appeals shall be as provided by law.

Section 10. Repealed.

Section 11. Repealed.

Section 12. Removal of State Capital

The seat of government of the state shall not be removed or relocated without the assent of a majority of the electors of the state voting thereupon, at a general election or elections, under such rules and regulations as to the number of elections and manner of voting and places to be voted for, as may be prescribed by law. Provided the question of removal may be submitted at such other general elections as may be provided by law.

Section 13. Labor Organizations; No Denial of Employment; Closed Shop Not Permitted

No person shall be denied employment because of membership in or affiliation with, or resignation or expulsion from a labor organization or because of refusal to join or affiliate with a labor organization; nor shall any individual or corporation or association of any kind enter into any contract, written or oral, to exclude persons from employment because of membership in or nonmembership in a labor organization.

Section 14. Labor Organization; Definition

The term "labor organization" means any organization of any kind, or any agency or employee representation committee or plan, which exists for the purpose, in whole or in part, of dealing with employers concerning grievances, labor disputes, wages, rates of pay, hours of employment, or conditions of work.

Section 15. Labor Organizations; Amendment Self-Executing; Laws to Facilitate Operation Permitted

This article is self-executing and shall supersede all provisions in conflict therewith; legislation may be enacted to facilitate its operation but no law shall limit or restrict the provisions hereof.

Section 16. Repealed.

Section 17. Retirement and Pension Funds; Investment

Notwithstanding section 3 of Article XIII or any other provision in the Constitution:

(1) The Legislature may provide for the investment of any state funds, including retirement or pension funds of state employees and Nebraska school employees in such manner and in such investments as it may by statute provide; and

(2) The Legislature may authorize the investment of retirement or pension funds of cities, villages, school districts, public power districts, and other governmental or political subdivisions in such manner and in such investments as the governing body of such city, village, school district, public power district and other governmental or political subdivision may determine but subject to such limitations as the Legislature may by statute provide.

Section 18. Governmental Powers and Functions; Intergovernmental Cooperation; Legislature May Limit; Merger or Consolidation of Counties or Other Local Governments Authorized

(1) The state or any local government may exercise any of its powers or perform any of its functions, including financing the same, jointly or in cooperation with any other governmental entity or entities, either within or without the state, except as the Legislature shall provide otherwise by law.

(2) The Legislature may provide for the merger or consolidation of counties or other local governments. No merger or consolidation of municipalities or counties shall occur without the approval of a majority of the people voting in each municipality or county to be merged or consolidated as provided by law. If the proposal is a merger or consolidation of one or more municipalities with one or more counties, the vote shall be tabulated in each municipality in the county or counties separately from the areas of the county or counties outside the boundaries of the municipalities. If the merger or consolidation is not approved by a majority of voters voting in the election in a municipality proposed to be merged or consolidated or the areas of the county or counties outside the boundaries of such municipality or municipalities, the proposed merger or consolidation shall be deemed rejected. Any merger or consolidation of local governments may be initiated by petition as provided by law. Annexation shall not be considered a merger or consolidation for purposes of this section. If the Legislature provides for the merger or consolidation of one or more municipalities with one or more counties, the Legislature shall provide for the reversal of the merger or consolidation. No such reversal shall occur without voter approval. The vote shall be tabulated in each municipality which is proposed to be created by the reversal separately from the areas outside the boundaries of the proposed municipalities. If the reversal is not approved by a majority of voters voting in the election in the area within the boundaries of any proposed municipality or the areas outside the proposed municipalities, the reversal shall be deemed rejected.

Section 19. Liquor Licenses; Municipalities and Counties; Powers

Notwithstanding any other provision of this Constitution, the governing bodies of municipalities and counties are empowered to approve, deny, suspend, cancel, or revoke retail and bottle club liquor licenses within their jurisdictions as authorized by the Legislature.

Sections 20-24. Omitted.

Article XVI: Amendments

Section 1. How Proposed

The Legislature may propose amendments to this Constitution. If the same be agreed to by three-fifths of the members elected to the Legislature, such proposed amendments shall be entered on the journal, with yeas and nays, and published once each week for three consecutive weeks, in at least one newspaper in each county, where a newspaper is published, immediately preceding the next election of members of the Legislature or a special election called by the vote of four-fifths of the members elected to the Legislature for the purpose of submitting such proposed amendments to the electors. At such election said amendments shall be submitted to the electors for approval or rejection upon a ballot separate from that upon which the names of candidates appear. If a majority of the electors voting on any such amendment adopt the same, it shall become a part of this Constitution, provided the votes cast in favor of such amendment shall not be less than thirty-five per cent of the total votes cast at such election. When two or more amendments are submitted at the same election, they shall be so submitted as to enable the electors to vote on each amendment separately.

Section 2. Convention

When three-fifths of the members elected to the Legislature deem it necessary to call a convention to revise, amend, or change this constitution, they shall recommend to the electors to vote at the next election of members of the Legislature, for or against a convention, and if a majority of the electors voting on the proposition, vote for a convention, the Legislature shall, at its next session provide by law for calling the same; Provided, the votes cast in favor of calling a convention shall not be less than thirty-five per cent of the total votes cast at such election. The convention shall consist of not more than one hundred members, the exact number to be determined by the Legislature, and to be nominated and elected from districts in the manner to be prescribed by the Legislature. Such members shall meet within three months after their election, for the purpose aforesaid. No amendment or change of this constitution, agreed upon by such convention, shall take effect until the same has been submitted to the electors of the state, and adopted by a majority of those voting for and against the same.

Article XVII: Schedule

Section 1. Terms; Reference to Members of the Legislature to Include Appointed and Elected Members

Whenever they shall appear in this Constitution, the terms members of the Legislature, elected members of the Legislature, or similar terms referring to the members of the Legislature, shall include appointed and elected members of the Legislature.

Section 2. Repealed.

Section 3. Repealed.

Section 4. General Election of State

The general election of this state shall be held on the Tuesday succeeding the first Monday of November in the year 1914 and every two years thereafter. All state, district, county, precinct, township and other officers, by the constitution or laws made elective by the people, except school district officers, and municipal officers in cities, villages and towns, shall be elected at a general election to be held as aforesaid. An incumbent of any office shall hold over until his successor is duly elected and qualified.

Section 5. Terms of Office of All Elected Officers

Unless otherwise provided by this Constitution or by law the terms of all elected officers shall begin on the first Thursday after the first Tuesday in January next succeeding their election.

Section 6. Transferred to Article III, section 30, Constitution of Nebraska.

Section 7. Repealed.

Section 8. Repealed.

Section 9. Repealed.

Section 10. Failed to carry at election.

Section 11. Repealed .

Article XVIII: Term Limits on Congress

Section 1. Statement of Intent

The people of the State of Nebraska want to amend the United States Constitution to establish term limits on Congress that will ensure representation in Congress by true citizen lawmakers. The President of the United States is limited by the XXII Amendment to the United States Constitution to two terms in office. Governors in forty states are limited to two terms or less. Voters have established term limits for over two thousand state legislators as well as over seventeen thousand local officials across the country. Nevertheless, Congress has ignored our desire for term limits not only by proposing excessively long terms for its own members but also by utterly refusing to pass an amendment for genuine congressional term limits. Congress has a clear conflict of interest in proposing a term limits amendment to the United States Constitution. A majority of both Republicans and Democrats in the 104th Congress voted against a constitutional amendment containing the term limits passed by a wide margin of Nebraska voters. The people, not Congress, should set term limits. We hereby establish as the official position of the citizens and State of Nebraska that our elected officials should enact by constitutional amendment congressional term limits of three terms in the United States House of Representatives and of two terms in the United States Senate. The career politicians dominating Congress have a conflict of interest that prevents Congress from being what the founders intended, the branch of government closest to the people. The politicians have refused to heed the will of the people for term limits; they have voted to dramatically raise their own pay; they have provided lavish million-dollar pensions for themselves; and they have granted themselves numerous other privileges at the expense of the people. Most importantly, members of Congress have enriched themselves while running up huge deficits to support their spending. They have put the government nearly $5,000,000,000,000.00 (five trillion dollars) in debt, gravely threatening the future of our children and grandchildren.

The corruption and appearance of corruption brought about by political careerism is destructive to the proper functioning of the first branch of our representative government. Congress has grown increasingly distant from the people of the states. The people have the sovereign right and compelling interest in creating a citizen Congress that will more effectively protect our freedom and prosperity. This interest and right may not effectively be served in any way other than that proposed by this initiative.

We hereby state our intention on behalf of the people of Nebraska, that this initiative lead to the adoption of the following amendment to the United States Constitution:

Congressional Term Limits Amendment to the United States Constitution

Section 1. No person shall serve in the office of United States Representative for more than three terms, but upon ratification of this amendment no person who has held the office of United States Representative or who then holds the office shall serve for more than two additional terms.

Section 2. No person shall serve in the office of United States Senator for more than two terms, but upon ratification of this amendment no person who has held the office of United States Senator or who then holds the office shall serve for more than one additional term.

Section 3. This article shall have no time limit within which it must be ratified to become operative upon the ratification of the legislatures of three-fourths of the several states.
Therefore, we the people of the State of Nebraska, have chosen to amend the Constitution of Nebraska to inform voters regarding incumbent and nonincumbent federal and state candidates' support for the congressional term limits amendment provided for in this section.

Section 2. Instruction to Members of Congressional Delegation; Ballot Notation; When

(1) We, the voters of Nebraska, hereby instruct each member of our congressional delegation to use all of his or her delegated powers to pass the congressional term limits amendment set forth in Article XVIII, section 1, of this Constitution.

(2) All primary and general election ballots shall have printed the information "DISREGARDED VOTERS INSTRUCTION ON TERM LIMITS" adjacent to the name of any United States Senator or United States Representative who:

(a) Fails to vote in favor of the proposed congressional term limits amendment set forth in Article XVIII, section 1, of this Constitution, when brought to a vote;

(b) Fails to second such proposed congressional term limits amendment if it lacks for a second before any proceeding of the legislative body;

(c) Fails to propose or otherwise bring to a vote of the full legislative body such proposed congressional term limits amendment if it otherwise lacks a legislator who so proposes or brings to a vote of the full legislative body such proposed congressional term limits amendment;

(d) Fails to vote in favor of all votes bringing such proposed congressional term limits amendment before any committee or subcommittee of the respective house upon which he or she serves;

(e) Fails to reject any attempt to delay, table, or otherwise prevent a vote by the full legislative body of such proposed congressional term limits amendment;

(f) Fails to vote against any proposed constitutional amendment that would establish longer term limits than those in the proposed congressional term limits amendment set forth in Article XVIII, section 1, of this Constitution, regardless of any other actions in support of such proposed congressional term limits amendment;

(g) Sponsors or cosponsors any proposed constitutional amendment or law that would increase term limits beyond those in the proposed congressional term limits amendment set forth in Article XVIII, section 1, of this Constitution; or

(h) Fails in any way to ensure that all votes on congressional term limits are recorded and made available to the public.

(3) The information "DISREGARDED VOTERS INSTRUCTION ON TERM LIMITS" shall not appear adjacent to the names of incumbent candidates for Congress if the congressional term limits amendment set forth in Article XVIII, section 1, of this Constitution, is before the states for ratification or has become part of the United States Constitution.

Section 3. Nonincumbent Candidates; Term Limits Pledge; Ballot Notation; When

(1) Nonincumbent candidates for the United States Senate, the United States House of Representatives, and the Legislature should be given an opportunity to take a "Term Limits Pledge" regarding term limits each time they file to run for such offices. Any such person who declines to take the "Term Limits Pledge" shall have the information "DECLINED TO PLEDGE TO SUPPORT TERM LIMITS" printed adjacent to his or her name on every primary and general election ballot.

(2) The "Term Limits Pledge" shall be offered to nonincumbent candidates for the United States Senate, the United States House of Representatives, and the Legislature until a constitutional amendment which limits the number of terms of United States

Senators to no more than two and United States Representatives to no more than three has become part of our United States Constitution.

(3) The "Term Limits Pledge" that each nonincumbent candidate, set forth in subsections (1) and (2) of this section, shall be offered is as follows: I support term limits and pledge to use all my legislative powers to enact the proposed constitutional amendment to the United States Constitution set forth in Article XVIII, section 1, of this Constitution. If elected, I pledge to vote in such a way that the designation "DISREGARDED VOTERS INSTRUCTION ON TERM LIMITS" will not appear adjacent to my name.
.... Signature of Candidate[1]

Section 4. Instruction to Members of the Legislature; Ballot Notation; When

(1) We the voters of Nebraska, hereby instruct each member of the Legislature to use all of his or her delegated powers to pass an application pursuant to Article V of the United States Constitution as set forth in subsection (2) of this section, and to ratify, if proposed, the congressional term limits amendment set forth in Article XVIII, section 1, of this Constitution.

(2) Application: We, the people and the Legislature, due to our desire to establish term limits on Congress, hereby make application to Congress, pursuant to our power under Article V of the United States Constitution, to call a convention for proposing amendments to the United States Constitution.

(3) All primary and general election ballots shall have the information "DISREGARDED VOTERS INSTRUCTION ON TERM LIMITS" printed adjacent to the name of any respective member of the Legislature who:

(a) Fails to vote in favor of the application set forth in subsection

(2) of this section when brought to a vote;

(b) Fails to second the application if it lacks for a second;

(c) Fails to vote in favor of all votes bringing the application before any committee or subcommittee upon which he or she serves;

(d) Fails to propose or otherwise bring to a vote of the full legislative body the application if it otherwise lacks a legislator who so proposes or brings to a vote of the full legislative body the application;

(e) Fails to vote against any attempt to delay, table, or otherwise prevent a vote by the full legislative body on the application;

(f) Fails in any way to ensure that all votes on the application are recorded and made available to the public;

(g) Fails to vote against any change, addition, or modification to the application;

(h) Fails to vote in favor of the congressional term limits amendment if it is sent to the states for ratification; or

(i) Fails to vote against any term limits amendment with longer terms if such an amendment is sent to the states for ratification.

(4) The information "DISREGARDED VOTERS INSTRUCTION ON TERM LIMITS" shall not appear adjacent to the names of candidates for the Legislature as required by subdivisions (3)(a) through (3)(g) of this section if the State of Nebraska has made an application to Congress for a convention for proposing amendments to the United States Constitution pursuant to this initiative and such application has not been withdrawn or the congressional term limits amendment set forth in Article XVIII, section 1, of this Constitution, has been submitted to the states for ratification.

(5) The information "DISREGARDED VOTERS INSTRUCTION ON TERM LIMITS" shall not appear adjacent to the names of candidates for the Legislature as required by subdivisions (3)(h) and (3)(i) of this section if the State of Nebraska has ratified the proposed congressional term limits amendment set forth in Article XVIII, section 1, of this Constitution.

(6) The information "DISREGARDED VOTERS INSTRUCTION ON TERM LIMITS" shall not appear adjacent to the names of candidates for the Legislature as required by subdivisions (3)(a) through (3)(i) of this section if the proposed congressional term limits amendment set forth in Article XVIII, section 1, of this Constitution, has become part of the United States Constitution.

Section 5. Ballot Notation; Secretary of State; Duties; Appeal

(1) The Secretary of State shall be responsible to make an accurate determination as to whether a candidate for the United States Senate, the United States House of Representatives, or the Legislature shall have placed adjacent to his or her name on the election ballot the information "DISREGARDED VOTERS INSTRUCTION ON TERM LIMITS" or "DECLINED TO PLEDGE TO SUPPORT TERM LIMITS."

(2) The Secretary of State shall consider timely submitted public comments prior to making the determination required in subsection (1) of this section.

(3) The Secretary of State, in accordance with subsection (1) of this section, shall determine and declare what information, if any, shall appear adjacent to the name of each incumbent member of Congress if he or she was to be a candidate in the next election. In the case of United States Representatives and United States Senators, this determination and declaration shall be made in a fashion necessary to ensure the orderly printing of primary and general election ballots with allowance made for all legal action provided in subsections (5) and (6) of this section, and shall be based upon his or her action during his or her current term of office and any action taken in any concluded term, if such action was taken after the determination and declaration was made by the Secretary of State in a previous election. In the case of incumbent members of the Legislature, this determination and declaration shall be made not later than thirty days after the end of the regular session following each general election, and shall be based upon legislative action in the previous regular session.

(4) The Secretary of State shall determine and declare what information, if any, will appear adjacent to the names of nonincumbent candidates for Congress and the Legislature, not later than five business days after the deadline for filing for the office.

(5) If the Secretary of State makes the determination that the information "DISREGARDED VOTERS INSTRUCTION ON TERM LIMITS" or "DECLINED TO PLEDGE TO SUPPORT TERM LIMITS" shall not be placed on the ballot adjacent to the name of a candidate for the United States Senate, the United States House of Representatives, or the Legislature, any elector may appeal such decision within five business days to the Nebraska Supreme Court as an original action or shall waive any right to appeal such decision; in which case the burden of proof shall be upon the Secretary of State to demonstrate by clear and convincing evidence that the candidate has met the requirements set forth in this article and therefore should not have the information "DISREGARDED VOTERS INSTRUCTION ON TERM LIMITS" or "DECLINED TO PLEDGE TO SUPPORT TERM LIMITS" printed on the ballot adjacent to the candidate's name.

(6) If the Secretary of State determines that the information "DISREGARDED VOTERS INSTRUCTION ON TERM LIMITS" or "DECLINED TO PLEDGE TO SUPPORT TERM LIMITS" shall be placed on the ballot adjacent to a candidate's name, the candidate or any elector may appeal such decision within five business days to the Nebraska Supreme Court as an original action or shall waive any right to appeal such decision; in which case the burden of proof shall be upon the candidate or any elector to demonstrate by clear and convincing evidence that the candidate should not have the information "DISREGARDED VOTERS INSTRUCTION ON TERM LIMITS" or "DECLINED TO PLEDGE TO SUPPORT TERM LIMITS" printed on the ballot adjacent to the candidate's name.

(7) The Nebraska Supreme Court shall hear the appeal provided for in subsection (5) of this section and issue a decision within sixty days. The Nebraska Supreme Court shall hear the appeal provided for in subsection (6) of this section and issue a decision not later than sixty-one days before the date of the election.[1]

Section 6. Automatic Repeal; When

At such time as the congressional term limits amendment set forth in Article XVIII, section 1, of this Constitution, has become part of the United States Constitution, sections 1 through 6 of this article automatically shall be repealed.

Section 7. Legal Challenge; Jurisdiction.

Any legal challenge to this initiative shall be filed as an original action before the Nebraska Supreme Court.

Section 8. Severability

If any portion, clause, or phrase of this initiative is, for any reason, held to be invalid or unconstitutional by a court of competent jurisdiction, the remaining portions, clauses, and phrases shall not be affected, but shall remain in full force and effect.

www.ingramcontent.com/pod-product-compliance
Lightning Source LLC
Chambersburg PA
CBHW070142230526
45471CB00002B/479